BESTSELLER

Celia Brayfield's first novel, *Pearls* (1988), has sold over a million copies worldwide; her latter two, *White Ice* and *The Prince*, were UK top-ten bestsellers. She has written for *The Times*, the *Independent*, the *Sunday Telegraph*, the *Observer*, the *Sunday Express* and the *Spectator*, and contributed to radio and television programmes including Kaleidoscope, The Late Show and Woman's Hour.

Author photograph by Sasha Gusov

Also by Celia Brayfield

PEARLS

THE PRINCE

WHITE ICE

HARVEST

BESTSELLER
SECRETS OF SUCCESSFUL WRITING

CELIA BRAYFIELD

FOURTH ESTATE · London

First published in Great Britain in 1996 by
Fourth Estate Limited
6 Salem Road
London W2 4BU

10 9 8 7 6 5 4 3 2

A catalogue record for this book is available from the British
Library.

ISBN 1 85702 383 8

Typeset by Centracet Ltd, Cambridge
Printed in Great Britain by
Clay Ltd, St Ives plc

For Carmen

Contents

PART 1 HIT AND MYTH

PART 2 THE ART AND CRAFT

Contents

Contents

PART 3 AMBITION IN ACTION

Contents

Introduction

> Whenever a tale is told, it becomes night. No matter where the dwelling, no matter the time, no matter the season, the telling of tales causes a starry sky and a white moon to creep from the eaves and hover over the heads of the listeners. Sometimes, by the end of the tale, the chamber is filled with daybreak; other times a star shard is left behind, sometimes a ragged thread of storm sky. And whatever is left behind is our bounty to work with, to use toward soul-making.
>
> WOMEN WHO RUN WITH THE WOLVES
> *Clarissa Pinkola Estes*

This is a book about the technique of writing a bestseller – a great popular novel. It is also about the reasons why certain novels become bestsellers. It is also about the part which books play in our lives, because without understanding that an author may study all the technique in the world and never learn the secret of writing a great book.

This book is intended for the writer in everyone. It is mainly written for people who want to write, edit or publish popular fiction. Those who are intrigued by the bestseller mystique will find it illuminating, and if you read bestsellers you will read on with greater pleasure when you appreciate how they are written.

I believe that we all know by instinct what a story is and

how to tell it. This book is designed primarily to develop that instinct but also to explore the attitudes which block it. Writing a book is hard mental work; the skills are not difficult to master, but even so not everyone who can write a book can write a bestseller. We may be intimidated by ideals of literature, confused by opinions of what a bestseller ought to be, unable to get our own ideas in focus or uncertain of our ability with words. But we can learn.

As a child, I learned to tell jokes. I was a miserable little girl in a school 75% full of boys, and telling jokes was the only way to survive. At the age of ten I knew I wanted to write novels but was afraid I would never be good enough. Robert Louis Stevenson, I discovered, started his writing career as a journalist and since I liked his stories I decided to do likewise.

On newspapers I learned how to tell stories – well enough to hold the attention of our readers through a 1,000-word article and well enough to amuse my colleagues, which was more important. I became a film critic, then a television critic. Film fascinated me. So did the fact that television viewers, who my editors considered to be morons, could hold 35 storylines of a series in their heads for three months even if they missed half the episodes, or invent a complete story on the basis of a 45-second commercial while cooking dinner at the same time.

I wrote three non-fiction books, which had modest sales. Having written for half a million readers or more for my entire professional life, I saw no reason to narrow my horizons just because I was writing books. I helped other writers structure treatments, I researched and edited their novels. Then I wrote my first novel, *Pearls*. My agent remembers what the publisher said when she got the outline: 'This is the best synopsis I've ever read – Celia is a genius.'

Pearls has now sold over a million copies. A week before it appeared in paperback the publisher's sales director was passing through Manchester Airport and saw *Pearls* displayed in the bookshop. Annoyed, he found the manager and complained that the book was on sale before its publication date. 'You won't complain when I tell you we're selling one copy every two minutes,' the manager replied.

When I wrote that book I had never been formally taught to tell a story. I had picked up a few basic techniques, like the famous 'don't tell me, show me,' but most of what I knew, I knew by instinct. It was only when I felt like a 'real' writer that I began to attend lectures on writing. In the first seminar, which lasted a weekend, I understood by 11am on the Saturday morning why *Pearls* had been such a success.

To write this book, I analysed what I do when I write a novel. Because there is much comparison of methods among writers, I know that we are all different. What I find easy, others find hard; what I find awesomely clever, others find commonplace. There is a classical structure to most stories, which this book defines, but there is no one way to interpret it, only the way you choose. There is no one way to write a book, only the way that will work for you. This book is designed to help you find that way.

What is a Bestseller?

In numbers, a book which sells 100,000 copies or more can fairly be called a bestseller. Of the 8,000 new novels published every year, about a hundred will achieve these sales, with the same, or greater, foreign sales in addition. In this book, however, I have chosen illustrations from the cream of the crop, the one or two books each year which sell millions. With the exception of the latest titles, these books have been filmed or televised, sometimes several times over. They have been reprinted over and over again – the earliest of them, *Gone With The Wind*, has been constantly in print for 60 years.

You stay awake all night to finish a book like this, and then feel sad at the end because the book was like a lover and although it will now be your companion for life you will never again have the rose-tinted thrill of falling in love with it. Books like this are kept, treasured, read and re-read, eagerly loaned to friends, crammed into pockets, crushed into handbags, dropped in the bath, splattered with spaghetti sauce and repaired with Scotch tape when their spines are broken and their yellowed pages loose. Books like this are so loved that they can change our lives, shape our hopes, and fix our ambitions.

There are many books which have been inspired by or written in imitation of these great popular classics, and they too have been bestsellers. For technical purposes they may illustrate the principles of popular fiction perfectly well, but they are less well known and so less useful as examples. They may be good books, but they are not great books, not the stories which broke new ground, which first put into words the ideas which millions of people already had on their minds.

The Secret

Bestsellers are part of popular culture. The ideas which begin in books are translated into films or television, into video games and cartoons, into plays, musicals, radio shows and cabaret acts, into catchphrases, fashion concepts, toys and marketing campaigns, into children's rhymes and playground games.

Ideas move all the time between these different media, changing form as they circulate. In South Africa in 1995 the story was told of a group of children who, having no television and no money, used to beg for enough to buy one cinema ticket, which would then be given to the best storyteller among them so that he or she could see the film and come back to tell them about it.

Books are the seed-corn of popular culture. While the literary élite anticipates the death of the novel, books have become the medium in which tens of thousands of ideas are scattered – a few of them to take root in the collective imagination of the world.

The bestselling novel is the only medium through which a single artist can communicate directly with millions. Film, television and music are all collaborative, high-tech and high-cost processes in which the authentic voice of the individual is lost in a consensus, but a book remains one person's vision. In comparison with other media, books are absurdly cheap. Book publishing still has the room for experiment and for failure which is disappearing in the rest of mass culture. This unique connection between one person and millions, far more than the fabled riches of the bestselling author, is what makes writing a book an almost universal ambition.

All popular culture tells stories, and the stories which are told are about ideas which are important to very large numbers of people. They are stories which are superficially about fictional characters, invented places and fantastic scenarios, but which in fact are about ordinary life. They pretend to be nothing but entertainment, but in fact address the hopes and fears of the whole human race. They present themselves as modern stories, even stories about the future, but when analysed and compared with the literature of the past, they are revealed as very old stories; most of them have been told for as long as people have used language, certainly long before the invention of writing. They are myths.

We think of mythology as something which belongs to the past but, like the shapeshifting gods of our ancestors, it is always disguising itself. Mythology is not a collection of fairy stories told in primitive societies which disappeared as scientific knowledge advanced; mythology is a series of ideas which co-ordinates a living person with the cycle of life, which teaches the individual how to act, and society how to survive. Ancient mythology is a subject for academic study. Modern mythology is what entertains us on a Saturday night.

Joseph Campbell, who related mythology, anthropology and psychology in a series of books whose status is itself almost legendary, wrote that 'the material of myth is the material of our life, the material of our body and the material of our environment, and a living, vital mythology deals with these in terms that are appropriate to the nature of knowledge of the time' (*Transformations of Myth Through Time*, Harper & Row, 1990).

Campbell's work demonstrated three propositions which are of great significance for any artist who seeks a mass audience. Firstly, he showed that the mythological stories of all the ancient cultures correspond to each other, that they are all different interpretations of one cycle of tales. Secondly, building on the work of Freud and Jung, Campbell showed that this cycle of stories relates to the inner journey of self-knowledge which every individual makes in achieving maturity. And thirdly, he showed that myths change and develop as society changes and develops.

Ancient myths are concerned with the cosmos and the mystic dimension of creation, as well as the rites and wrongs of human life. So are modern myths. The stories which are told around the world are stories which hit a nerve in the collective unconscious, which externalise beliefs held by millions of people.

The inner content of these stories is wrapped up, as attractively as human skill can achieve, in an outer idea which is also significant for the audience. Michael Crichton's *Jurassic Park* is superficially about dinosaurs, really about our fear that in meddling with creation scientists will destroy the world. Robert Harris's *Fatherland* is superficially about Nazi Germany, really about our wish that whatever evil there is in the world may be overcome as long as one good person survives. John Grisham's *The Firm* is about the same wish. *The Bridges of Madison County* by Robert James Waller is superficially a rural love story about a farmer's wife and a freelance photographer, really a confirmation that love is sacred and worth any suffering.

In the oldest sense, storytelling is a healing art. It reconciles us to our anxieties and makes it possible for us to master them. It assures us that our values are right and that our lives will continue, and teaches us what we must do to find ourselves. It connects us to the archetypes which guide us through life.

In primitive societies stories were part of the rituals which initiated people into each successive passage of life, from birth to death. At each transition an old self was left behind, a new identity assumed, and a new role in society accepted. Religion no longer has the power to smooth these transitions for us. We have few rituals now, but many stories to teach us what lies ahead.

Stories are not literal exercises of the ideas that are on so many people's minds. If those thoughts could be addressed consciously, we would do so. Literary novels *are* able to approach these concepts directly as well as dramatising them in story form: in a literary novel the characters can pause to debate the morality of genetic engineering; in a popular novel, the raptors eat a baby.

The ideas which are rehearsed in stories are immense and frightening because they are too large for our conscious understanding. Bestsellers are often called 'escapist', and so they are – but what their readers are escaping from is not life, but the fear that they cannot understand life. Stories explain our lives in terms which we can accept.

Mythology cannot do its work in the open. Its first task is to persuade us to suspend disbelief, to surrender our cynicism, to open our hearts like children hearing a fairy tale or our ancestors gathered around their hearths. This is where the skills of storytelling are needed.

The Magic Formula

> There were two goats in the Mojave desert. They were starving; for days they had found nothing to eat. Then they found a tin of film. The bigger one nuzzled it until the lid came off. The film leader loosened around the spool and the big goat ate a few frames. The little goat tried to butt in and nibble the edge, but the big goat kicked him away and greedily ate the lot. When there was nothing left but the spool, the little goat looked enviously at his big companion and said, 'Well, what was it like?'
>
> 'It was good,' said the big goat, burping. 'But the book was better.'
>
> *adapted from* CLOSE-UP
> *Len Deighton*

A joke is a very short story. It has all the essential features: it happens in its own world – in this case a place where goats talk; it has conventions – in this case, that the little guy is the good guy; it takes our emotions for a ride and surprises us with what we expect – a punchline.

In the same way, a story has its own world, its own conventions, its own emotional profile and its own way of satisfying our expectations. These combine to create the form which encases the content of the story, the structure which makes the events related universally significant. This structure draws the readers' attention to what is important and entices them to pursue the story right to its end.

This book is about storytelling, not about literature. Literary writing can encompass storytelling, but does not value it. I have heard literary authors hiss with contempt at the mere words 'story structure'. Literary writing has developed a system of aesthetic values related to language, intellectual concepts and an appreciation of the literature of the past. Literary élitists believe that popular fiction must be badly written. This is not so. Popular fiction must be clearly written, something which is not required of literature. When a literary novel is clearly written, well-constructed and governed by an idea of large enough significance, it can become a bestseller, as witness *The Name of the Rose*, *The Good Mother* or *The Joy Luck Club*.

We learn the classical structure of a story before we learn the alphabet. It is a form common to drama and to literature. By the time we are adults our understanding of stories has been developed by television and film to a highly sophisticated level. Screenwriters study storytelling techniques in depth; authors do not. An author is thrilled with an audience of one million – to a screenwriter, one million is a negligible minority. Encouraged by literary culture, authors probably pay less attention to technique than artists in any other field.

For a writer, learning how to tell a great story is less a process of acquiring new knowledge than one of unearthing instinctive knowledge from beneath a mountain of fear, prejudice and ignorance.

Money

To everyone who is not on one, bestseller lists are not about writing, but about money. Authors like John Grisham and

Michael Crichton are supposed to rank among the wealthiest entertainers in the world, with annual incomes estimated in tens of millions of dollars. The bestseller seems less like a book than a piece of sorcery by which base words are turned into gold. The notion that a bestseller is created by inspiration, intelligence, skill, commitment and hard work is dismissed out of hand. The bestseller has become embedded in its own mythology of massive advances, mega-sales, formula writing, book doctors and super-agents. Nothing in this lurid mystique is of any assistance in writing a book, but it has made the ambition to do so immensely attractive. There is an apocryphal story that the central computer of the Foreign Office in London crashed because so many civil servants were writing novels on it that the system was overloaded. A BBC television programme recently ran a poll and discovered that one person in ten thinks they could write a book, and one in fifty has already done so.

The bestseller seems tantalisingly accessible. All that is needed is a pencil and paper. This book discusses the content of a story, research, narrative techniques and questions of style. It tells you how to motivate yourself and keep that motivation, and how to find a publisher. It tells you who your readers are and what they want in a book.

Anyone who can write believes, somewhere in their heart, that they could write a book, if only they had one extra thing: the time, the application, even just the plot. This book cannot give you those things; what it *will* do is tell you how other writers have found them.

PART
1

HIT AND MYTH

1

How Stories Work

'It has always been the function of mythology to supply the symbols that carry the human spirit forward.'

THE HERO WITH A THOUSAND FACES
Joseph Campbell

Storytelling is a way of explaining the world emotionally rather than analytically. Instead of reducing the world to verbal concepts and forming an argument from them, a story creates a model of the world and leads the reader into it, to have the experience of living at a comfortable scale in a magic ground where all action is symbolic. A story is a playground for the mind, a safe place where the reader can assume a fantasy identity and act out an imaginary drama. In this way the whole of life can be rehearsed, one scene at a time, either preparing for the events which lie ahead or resolving feelings about what has already happened. In ancient cultures, myths are inseparable from the rituals which act out their stories. We have always learned about life by dramatising our questions.

The model of life which a story builds is metaphorical. Some are made to look realistic, but the storyteller must take care to fix a sign over the entrance making it clear that this is a magic ground, a place removed from the world where rituals are enacted. Here the storyteller offers his audience wisdom which seems warmer and more solid than the cold, rickety constructions of reasoning. He allows them to make their own discoveries, which they will trust in preference to an external explanation. He enables them to rehearse their emotions, to become comfortable with them at the level of fantasy and so gain control of them in reality.

To be a bestseller, a book must succeed at three levels. At the emotional level it must offer the reader a satisfying experience. At the level of conscious thought, it must exercise a question about life which is already too large for the reader's mind. At the psychological level, it must take the reader on a journey towards a new life, a passage through destruction, fear and struggle to a higher level of consciousness.

A story is organic. It is born as a germ of an idea with the embryonic beginnings of all the necessary features to work successfully at all three levels. Writing a story is a process of allowing this germ to grow, and writing it effectively means developing it as a whole, with all its inter-dependent parts working powerfully together. In the second part of this book, we will define these elements and discover how they function: The *theme* and *central character* govern the way the story works psychologically, the *location* of the story rules its operation at the conscious level and the *narrative* dramatises the whole work and transforms it into an emotional experience for the reader.

The Narrative

The shape of a story is something which we discover as children and anticipate ever afterwards. A well-constructed story feels absolutely natural to its audience, because we are so familiar with its form. The technique of telling the story should be invisible, allowing the reader to enter the story completely and experience it emotionally.

At the start of a book, the author makes a pact with the reader, promising the experience which the reader is expecting. When the reader's conscious mind starts adding a critical commentary to the story – 'That would never happen', 'that can't be right', 'that's not true', 'yes, but what about . . .?' – the spell of the story is broken and the trust which the reader has placed in the author is destroyed. The reading stops and the story has failed.

Learning to construct a narrative means learning to make that pact and keep it. It means understanding the elements of a story, learning the techniques which make it lifelike and learning how to help your reader follow your thoughts. Like a circus acrobat, the author learns the tricks themselves, learns to make them look easy, and then adds the spangles and the flourishes and the hoopla which make the whole performance thrilling.

The Outer World

> 'Myths and fairy stories both answer the eternal questions: What is the world really like? How am I to live my life in it? How can I truly be myself?'
>
> THE USES OF ENCHANTMENT
> *Bruno Bettelheim*

Mythology is a way of integrating the individual with society. This is the conscious level of a story's function, one of which the readers are often aware and for which they will choose to read a particular story. At this level a story will be discussing morality and defining right and wrong, but never directly. Remember the wisdom of Sam Goldwyn: messages are for Western Union.

Stories have the power to process the thoughts which are too large for our mental equipment. We need this comfort as soon as our understanding is mature enough for us to be aware of what we do not know. Logic alone is not big enough for this job because it is itself a product of our understanding and the fears which have been aroused in us are already larger than that: science is uncontrollable, intolerance will destroy the world, modern morality will destroy society, evil will triumph, we have no power to save our lives – these anxieties are just as monstrous as the fears of childhood. They need big answers.

Consider the surreal world of a fairy story, beyond logic but corresponding to a child's understanding of the world as a wonderland of giant frights, arbitrary rules and unattainable delights. You can't reassure a scared child as well by arguing that monsters don't exist so there can't be one on top of the bedroom cupboard as you can by explaining that Spiderman has netted the monster and will be on guard by their bedside all night. That explanation works for the child because it addresses the fear in the terms in which it has appeared. If you ask the same child in daylight if Spiderman really exists, he'll say, 'Of course not, he's a cartoon. Everybody knows that.'

Integrating individuals into society is a process which has become more difficult as society changes at dizzying speed. A great many modern stories address the fears aroused by those changes. We do not now turn to mythology to explain the universe or creation; on these topics we are happy to accept the rational explanations of science. Instead we are uncertain about things which our ancestors never questioned – what it is to be a man or a woman, a father or mother, a son or daughter, how to create a family, how to love.

To discuss these questions, the storyteller selects a location in which the issues can be worked out clearly and strongly. How far that location is from real life largely depends on how much dynamite the issue contains – the more explosive, the further away. Genres of story grow up around the locations which hold significance for particular ideas, and as society's preoccupations shift so the locations shift and the genres develop. The skill of choosing a story's location is the skill of surfing the genres, of sensing the drift of a genre's development and the social shifts which underlie it.

The evolution of women's stories shows the process very clearly. One of the unique virtues of novels is that because they are read by individuals in private they can address one gender only. Unlike other mass media, they do not need to assume an audience made up of both men and women. A bestseller can sell the desired millions and still appeal to only one sex, which allows the discussion of issues which interest only one sex, and may even offend the other.

The change in the balance of power between men and

women is a social earthquake which is still happening. Census figures show that before World War II women accounted for only about a quarter of the workforce in the US and the UK; now that proportion has doubled. The biggest increase – more than five-fold – has been in the proportion of women in professional and managerial jobs. At the same time, the size of the average family has shrunk; there are more single parents, more only children and demographers predict that 15% of today's thirtysomethings will remain childless. Patricia Aburdene and John Naisbitt, authors of the *Megatrends* analyses of social trends, define 'seismic economic and social implications' in five areas: in employment patterns, in management methods, in the family, in relationships and in individual self-image.

The bestsellers bought by our generation show these ideas in debate. As a critical mass of public opinion develops around an issue, a genre of writing appears to dramatise it. *Gone With The Wind* in 1938 put a century between its readers and the question of women at work, and substituted the social chaos of post-Revolutionary Georgia for the social upheaval of America after the Depression:

Frank would never forget the horror of that moment. Go into business for herself! It was unthinkable. There were no women in business in Atlanta. In fact, Frank had never heard of a woman in business anywhere ... for a woman to leave the protection of her home and venture out into the rough world of men, competing with them in business, rubbing shoulders with them, being exposed to insult and gossip ... Especially when she wasn't forced to do it, when she had a husband amply able to provide for her!

The issue went underground during World War II, after which a plethora of period romances appeared in which the heroine's position was one of absolute powerlessness. The worlds created by Georgette Heyer and Catherine Cookson were men's worlds, and their heroines among the most disadvantaged of citizens, being not only female but usually poor and sometimes directly under the control of the leading man as his ward or employee. Germaine Greer observed that in Georgette Heyer's books, 'The utterly ineffectual heroine is the most important part of the story.'

The classic romance story appeals to the sense of powerlessness which many women still feel. It reassures them that they will survive in this world without being able to control it, and that the power which they lack lies in the hands of men who are benevolent. This question too needed more than a century of distance before it could be addressed.

The major shock of the social earthquake was the sexual revolution of the Sixties. It was narrowly predated by the appearance of a different kind of heroine in period stories like *Forever Amber* (1948) and *Angelique* (1959), heroines who sought economic independence and were also actively sexual, still such disturbing figures that they had to be contemplated at a distance of at least three hundred years. Not until Jackie Collins wrote *The World Is Full of Married Men* in 1968 could such a figure appear successfully in a modern story, located in the nightclub underworld of London. Like the heroines of Jacqueline Susann, this woman was such a disturbing figure that she had to come to a bad end. She was succeeded by *The Bitch*, who got away with sexual and economic power but was viewed as an almost pornographic creation.

The central character of Colleen McCullough's *The Thorn Birds*, from 1977, has ambitions only for a home and a family. In a story which shifted the domestic dilemma of millions of women to the Australian outback, Meggie Cleary destroys not only her own happiness but also the man she loves through an obsessive passion which has no counterbalance. In that year in the US, two million businesses were owned by women.

The issue suddenly came into sharp focus, in a world only just over the horizon of everyday life. The working woman appeared triumphant in Judith Krantz's *Scruples* in 1979, set in the contemporary and highly aspirational world of high-fashion retailing. She was swiftly followed by Barbara Taylor Bradford's *A Woman of Substance*, which married the business woman to the family saga. Love stories suddenly ceased to be period romances and the contemporary stories of Danielle Steele appeared, whose heroines are ordinary middle-class women who balance their working and emotional lives.

While these new genres developed, between 1980 and 1988, the number of female entrepreneurs in the US grew by 82%, and the revenue they generated grew by 129%. Thirty per cent of all new businesses started by women in the UK are in retailing. The US Small Business Association predicts that 40% of small firms will be owned by women by the year 2000, and in some sectors women in the workforce already outnumber men.

The bestseller lists have witnessed the anxieties let loose in this process. There is the deep unease of Dr Kay Scarpetta, Patricia Cornwall's brilliant, divorced, childless forensic investigator. There have been backlash stories like *The Silence of the Lambs, Disclosure* and *Presumed Innocent* in which women have suffered because they ventured too far into men's worlds. And now that the dust is settling, male writers have become interested in emotional issues. *The Bridges of Madison County* and Nicholas Evans' *The Horse Whisperer*, stories which go out to the wilderness in search of wisdom, are the first love stories written by men to reach a mass readership for over twenty years.

The process overall demonstrates how a new world develops a new mythology to work through its concerns, and how different societies chose different locations as the setting for the discussion. The bestsellers of the day are those books which not only pick up the questions facing society but find the arena in which they can rehearse those issues with the best effect.

The Inner Story

At the psychological level, every story is about rebirth. Stories dramatise the progress of all rites of passage – separation–initiation–return – by showing the transformation of one individual (or, rarely, a pair or group of individuals) through a series of trials. This is the *heroic journey*, whose elements are common to the mythology of every age and culture. It is a quest, a search for a new self. In *Fatherland*, a police detective in Nazi Germany is transformed from an alienated non-combatant into a hero who risks his life to challenge the state. In Daphne du Maurier's *Rebecca*, an inadequate girl jealous of her husband's glamorous first wife grows into a confident woman. In *Shogun* by James Clavell, a sixteenth-century English sailor moves from ignorance to enlightenment through contact with Japanese culture. In J G Ballard's *The Empire of the Sun*, a boy grows up in wartime Shanghai.

These are wide-screen adventures played for high stakes. Our own lives are adventures with the same scenario of transformation, but achieved internally. At each stage of our lives we are challenged to change, to leave behind the conscious and unconscious attitudes of the phase which is passing and assume a new role and new responsibilities. Stories help us to do this. One of the most perceptive compliments I ever received was from a painter who wrote, 'You write stories about grown-ups growing up.'

Life itself is a constant cycle of dying to the old and being reborn in a new identity. Like ancient rituals and the mythology which they dramatised, stories help to lead people safely across the successive thresholds of maturity.

The stories circulated in all popular culture work at the same three levels, but the novel explores the psychological most deeply. Only in a book can the audience enter the thoughts of the characters and sense the evolution of their souls from the inside. This is why so many of us can agree with Len Deighton's goat and say, 'The book was better.' Many films and television series have an unsatisfying psychological dimension because the characters do not develop, or develop so slowly that the audience cannot experience the process; they are challenged only to stay the same. The most obvious example is James Bond, created in *Casino Royale* by Ian Fleming as a human character full of inner conflicts but translated in films as a symbolic figure fighting external battles only.

The Source

Myths come from the unconscious wells of fantasy in our minds. Joseph Campbell, building on the work of Jung and his followers, noted that when people are working through experiences in psychoanalysis they will sometimes have dreams which correspond closely to the mythological stories of primitive cultures with which they have never had any contact.

Telling stories to make sense of the world is something which developed with human intelligence itself. Mythology is as old as our species – it dates from the time of early *Homo sapiens*, Neanderthal man, 200,000 BC to 40,000 BC when the first traces of burial rituals and cave-bear worship tell us that our ancestors had a mythological explanation for life and death. The following Cro-Magnon era in Europe, from the western shores of France to Lake Baikal, has left us the Venus figures which express our ancestors' ideas about fertility. The Lascaux cave paintings show how storytelling added mystical significance to the daily lives of those who first gazed on them. All these images reappear spontaneously in the mythological art of unrelated cultures all over the world.

Mythology is constantly evolving. The creation stories of prehistory evolved into the foundation myths of world religions. The gods and heroes of ancient cultures became the knights and ladies of poetry, the kings and queens of legend, the saints of religion. *Cinderella*, as Marina Warner has shown (*From The Beast To The Blonde*, Chatto and Windus, 1994), is a very old story. Her earliest written appearance was in China around AD 850. Her story was a fashionable entertainment when Charles Perrault published it in his fairy tale collection in eighteenth-century Paris, and while the orphan girl, the pumpkin and the fairy godmother now belong to the nursery and Walt Disney, the story's themes of transformation, female rivalry and motherlessness reappear throughout modern culture – in *Wild Swans* and *The Joy Luck Club*, in *Scruples* and *Pearls*, in films as disparate as *Working Girl*, *Pretty Woman* and *Raise The Red Lantern*.

Your Story and You

Writers often have a sense that their story chose them, rather than the other way around. In collecting folk tales, Clarissa Estes observed that the best storytellers seemed to have grown from their stories, like trees from a root. In developing a story, the writer himself sets out on an inner journey, answering his own questions and healing his own wounds as he works.

This is not an easy progress. It is much more comfortable to sit home by the fire than to set out on an adventure into the unknown. It is much more pleasant to splash around in the shallows of entertaining other people than to dive deep into the process of discovering yourself. However, it is much better for you and for your readers to take the harder path. Writers I know who persistently avoid their own conflicts produce very nice books which lack compulsion. They are technically accomplished but there seems to be no reason why anyone should read them.

Because writing a story demands this inner struggle, it is a process which has particular difficulties. Writers are encouraged to dread being 'blocked' but not taught the techniques of self-motivation which will carry them through the rough patches. The third part of this book discusses these techniques and examines the motivational problems of writing.

In many cases the difference between wanting to write a book and actually doing it is only having the will to begin. 'Nobody ever wants to start,' is the most useful piece of advice I was ever given about motivation. A very gifted trainer helped me stumble through my first run, congratulated me, gave me a high five and then said, 'Next time you come to do this, you won't want to start. That's normal. I've trained all kinds of people up to Olympic athletes and we're all the same. None of us ever wants to start. *I* don't want to start. I run every day and I never want to start. So when you don't want to start, remember this conversation. Then get going.'

Your Readers

No intimate relationship is approached with less thought than that between a writer and a reader. When someone is gripped by a book and spends a whole weekend, or half his holiday or all his free time in a month reading it to the end, he is enjoying a one-to-one conversation with the author. It is the longest and probably also the deepest conversation of his life at the time, one of those late-night life-art-and-the-meaning-of-existence conversations. What the reader says in that conversation remains in his own mind, where he constantly questions, explores or agrees with what he is reading. The process is enthralling and exhausting, and he will complete it with an almost euphoric sense of order in the universe and satisfaction with his own place in it.

Thinking of a book as a conversation helps to keep the writer aware of the reader and of the skills involved in sustaining their dialogue. The social skills needed to carry on a long discussion are sophisticated; we acquire them in early adolescence, through the process of questioning the world whose awesome dimensions we are discovering. We learn how to interest people in our ideas, how to relate one point to the next, how to win the respect of our listeners, how to hold their attention, how to use shock, humour, aggression or fantasy to colour our arguments.

Some people never learn these skills. Sustaining a dialogue is impossible for them because they cannot empathise with their listeners or pick up the signs of their interest. Every community has them, the egomaniacs, the bores, the obsessives, the mumbling nerds. Through nervousness, self-obsession or insensitivity, they can only transmit communications, not receive them. Writers who lack a strong sense of their readers risk becoming one of these pariahs.

Deep conversations begin with curiosity, about the order of the world as well as about the other person and the contents of their mind. In talking we also expect to bring our own thoughts out into the open and define them, as well as learning from other speakers. We engage and keep the other's interest, advance opinions in relation to theirs, recap important points, and when the conversation breaks off, because one party has to answer the phone or open another bottle, we work to re-establish it. A bestseller is written in the same way, setting up a long dialogue with the reader, holding their attention, making sure the thread of the argument is never broken.

Most successful authors have a very strong sense that when they write they are in communication with a *someone*. They have an inner reader constantly responding to their words. That inner reader is not defined in demographic terms – their age, gender, education, lifestyle and disposable income are not part of the picture. The inner reader functions emotionally, giving the author a gut feeling for how the story is being heard. Authors will express this sense by saying they write for themselves, because their inner reader is formed instinctively, not consciously or logically defined.

In fact, that instinct has been trained. I trained mine telling jokes to ten-year-old boys, the only way I could find to stop them pulling my hair and putting worms down the neck of my school dress. As an adult, my instinct was trained on newspapers where editors threw our stories back at us after the first paragraph if they were bored. Sometimes they got sophisticated and hurled a 'page-traffic survey' after it: 100% of readers turn to your page, 95% look at the picture, 60% begin your article, 3% finish it. *Three per cent.* All those painfully extracted facts, all that meticulously constructed argument, all that sweat and agony, the frightfully clever joke in the second column and only three per cent of the folks out there get to hear the whole story. Imagine an 800-seat theatre with only one row filled.

The majority of bestselling authors have worked in professions which depend on communication, in the media, teaching or politics. All communication is a two-way street, an interaction between speaker and listener in which an effective speaker picks up the signs that the listeners are paying attention and adapts her material to keep them enthralled. If you have not developed these reactions before you come to write a book, you will lack the ability to judge the impact of your own work.

The best communicators have a deep respect for their audience. Whether their approach is dominating or co-operative, they view the audience as equals. They are completely committed to the achievement of the audience's understanding and never for one moment believe that they have the right to put their own needs above those of their listeners.

Disrespect for the audience is sudden death. In performers it is the quickest way to empty the house. People will not stay to be disparaged, and certainly will not maintain a commitment to a long and complicated story if it is giving them even the subtlest sense that they are being treated as inferior beings.

Meet Your Readers

While nothing can replace the process of learning to communicate on your feet, many writers could benefit from a keener appreciation of who their readers are and under what circumstances they are reading. To make this introduction properly, I conducted a survey. From talking to people who read all kinds of popular fiction as well as people who read my books – who also write me letters – I approached this task with an idea of how popular fiction is read, and who reads it. To find a sample of them I sent out a hundred questionnaires through ten outlets: a design group, an estate agency, a bank, a firm of accountants, a health club, a dentists' association, a sixth-form college, a post-graduate college, and a choral society.

The questionnaire was designed to find a self-selected sample of regular readers, and to probe attitudes and habits rather than count heads. Spontaneous comments were welcomed.

Popular fiction readers are you and me. They belong to the mass middle class, which means that they are intelligent, well-educated, well-informed, hard-working, curious and aware. You can be sure that some of your readers will know as much, if not more, about your subject than you do:

✔ 77% of the questionnaire respondents completed full-time education at the age of 18 or over, 46% finishing or planning to finish at over the age of 21.

✔ Their occupations: accountants, actors, administrators, bankers, bank clerks, beauty therapist, designers, estate agents, a hairdresser, lecturers, lawyers, managers, orthodontists, secretaries, students, supervisors, a surveyor, a tai chi master, a telephonist, a translator and a xerox operator.

One of the most important things to appreciate about the world in which you are writing is that it demands a very particular form of intelligence. In writing for millions, you will be addressing hundreds of thousands of people who are clever but not necessarily clever with words. The highly verbal way of thinking which writers develop naturally in using their gifts is not universal, nor is it a measure of general intelligence. A painter, a mathematician or a pianist can have a brilliant mind but very little facility with words. I have known photographers of international acclaim who could barely write their own invoices. While some of the people who open your book will tear through it in a day, others may take a week and will appreciate your skill in holding their attention:

✔ the majority of respondents, 64%, described themselves as average readers. Only 30% considered that they were fast readers.

Another factor to consider is that our society is multi-cultural, multi-ethnic and increasingly multi-lingual. A book which sells millions will be marketed all over the world, and many of your readers will not read it in their first language.

In the population at large, reading is not a growing skill. Literacy levels have not risen since World War II, and some studies show that they are declining. Almost fifteen per cent of the general population has limited literacy, according to a survey conducted in 1995 by the National Commission on Education.

Book Lovers

People love to read. They want to read more than they do. They look back wistfully on their youth, when they read more, and look forward to being older and having more leisure time to spend with books. Even if they can only manage to read four books a year, they will read anywhere, while doing anything. When not reading a book, they will read newspapers or magazines. One respondent said only an earthquake would make her abandon a book once she had begun it. Older respondents said that only losing their eyesight would make them stop.

People who like to read will read anything. They are omnivorous. The respondents' preferences included novels and non-fiction, classics, literary fiction and popular fiction, plays, murder mysteries, horror, humour, biography, romance, histories, sagas, action stories, gossip, modern culture, poetry and works on religion or philosophy. They can be loyal: when they find an author they like they will read everything by that author, and the writers whose work was read in that serial fashion ranged from Charles Dickens and Thomas Hardy to Sidney Sheldon and Catherine Cookson.

People acquire books by many different means, buying them new or second-hand, borrowing them from friends or library. Heavy borrowers own fewer books. They are easily tempted:

✔ 90% want to read for pleasure more than they do

✔ 64% read more when they were younger

✔ 84% expect to read more when they are older

✔ 89% also read magazines for pleasure, 75% read newspapers

✔ 11% own over 1,000 books, 57% own over 100

✔ 55% have bought a book to read for pleasure in the past month, 84% have bought a book in the past year

✔ 58% of those books were bought in a large bookstore

✔ 53% of all the books bought were impulse purchases

Serial Readers

Most popular-fiction readers become interested in an author they like and will want to read other books they have written. By far the most compelling reason for buying a book – cited as first or second in importance in the decision to buy by 98% of the respondents – was liking the author's other books. The same number had a favourite author or had read several books by the same author. Writing means establishing a long relationship with your readers, a relationship which will continue as long as you can hold their interest.

Time Poverty

> An hour is something you can work with. You can go jogging or play with your children or take a nap or read a book in an hour.
>
> WHAT THEY STILL DON'T TEACH YOU AT HARVARD
> BUSINESS SCHOOL
> *Mark H. McCormack*

Reading is almost by definition something which people do not have enough time for. In a life which is full and crammed with choices, reading is a luxury. Notice the priorities in Mark McCormack's advice above – health and family first, reading last. After work, most people's priorities are relational, they want to be with their families and friends, and to enjoy social occasions. They will allow themselves to read when their work is done and their responsibilities taken care of, when there is no more urgent entertainment to tempt them. Of the respondents:

✔ all were working full-time, either outside or inside the home, even the 7% past the age of retirement

✔ only 15% lived alone, the rest lived with partners, families or friends. Those who lived with young children included some of the heaviest readers.

✔ on average, reading was rated fifth in a list of leisure activities, with family, friends, films, theatre or concerts above it

✔ reading is a holiday pleasure for most people – 75% read on holiday

✔ 47% read at home at night, 41% whenever they have nothing to do, 49% at the weekend

✔ 'No time' or 'having work to do' was the second most common external reason for putting down a book

✔ 23% read 4–8 books a year, 29% manage to read between 12 and 20 books a year. The very light readers were the most senior and most junior members of their professions.

Print Junkies

There are professions which are notoriously print-intensive. A lawyer friend who was delighted to be given a role in the defence of the captain of a ship involved in a collision on the River Thames was less enthusiastic when the firm ordered an entire room to be cleared to store the documents – each member of the team had to read them all.

The law is an extreme case, but the truth is that most professions bring a pile of paper with them. Most people have enough to read already. By the time they get around to reading for pleasure their eyes are already swimming with words:

✔ 80% have at least one hour a day of professional reading to complete

✔ 51% said they sometimes felt they had too much professional reading, that they couldn't take it in or read everything that they should. 28% said they often felt this way.

✔ some people are completely bombed out with print, and the condition is no respecter of status. Among the questionnaire respondents were a college lecturer who estimated having more than 20 hours of reading a week and a reception manager with two hours' reading a day.

People who are overloaded with professional reading still want to read books. One of the main findings of a survey of students by *Cosmopolitan* magazine was the astonishing appetite for print of the respondents, 85% of whom were women aged 19–24. As well as their course books, they read an average of eleven books for pleasure each year, one third of them also read a daily newspaper and by definition all of them were magazine readers.

Pressure

The days when people gathered around the fireside after dinner every night to read aloud to each other have passed. One family in a million goes further than reading children a bedtime story. One person in a million has the time, in their normal day-to-day life, to spend a whole afternoon curled up with a book. Most people have to read when and where they can. Although it should not be necessary to point this out, many authors still write as if their every word was going to be reverently received by a public gathered docilely at their feet, willing to sacrifice the rest of their lives to understanding the author's matchless thoughts. If the great nineteenth-century writers constructed their vivid, flowing stories for people who were reading aloud in a group by the fireside, consider how much harder a twentieth-century writer has to work to hold the attention of people reading by themselves on the bus.

People who want to read have to do it against the interruptions of the world. They will not be alone for long and they will never be undisturbed – they probably read for, at most, half an hour at a stretch. Their attention span will be short, their concentration fragmented. They will be accustomed to other media which accept these limitations – particularly television, in which soap-opera scenes can last less than a minute. Jerzy Kosinski estimated that the average concentration span of a TV viewer was 25 seconds.

It is extremely likely that your readers will be tired. Because reading is an activity which is enjoyed but not felt to be justified when there are more urgent things to do, it is not scheduled for prime time. Most people read in bed at night, and 'tiredness' or 'falling asleep' is the most common external reason given for stopping.

People also read while doing other things. In this survey, it was particularly true of the heaviest readers that they seemed always to have a book in their hands, whatever they were doing:

✔ 77% read in bed at night

✔ All of those travelling to work by public transport read while travelling

✔ 62% read while doing something else

✔ all those with small children read while supervising them

✔ 60% read on long journeys

✔ 36% read while listening to music

✔ 25% read while eating

✔ 17% read while watching TV

✔ 23% read in the bath

✔ 4% read in traffic jams

When Reading Stops

Readers begin a book with a commitment to finishing it. The only thing which can interfere with that commitment is your failure as an author to hold their attention. While tiredness and pressure of other responsibilities were the biggest external reasons given for stopping reading, a wealth of factors in the book itself were cited, including being bored, finding the plot slow, not feeling one's imagination being caught, not being gripped by the first chapter, not believing the plot, not believing or liking the characters, not understanding the action or finding it too complex.

If you want your readers to finish your book, you have to help them. Only you can make sure that they hear the whole story.

Understanding how people read and the place that reading has in their lives is the beginning of understanding how to write for them. The craft techniques of popular fiction have developed to help a reader who is intelligent, curious, committed and alert for the pleasure that will enable them to overcome distractions and tiredness and follow the story to the end.

Readerism

Mickey Spillane said he had no fans, only customers. For a popular author it is important to develop an inner reader to oppose that attitude, which can still be found throughout all print media. The notion that the readers are the suckers and that the goal is to persuade them to buy a product which is inherently worthless amounts to 'readerism', a prejudice as irrational as sexism or racism.

Readerists are always briefing their writers with sweeping generalisations: 'Readers won't read description', or 'Readers aren't interested in ideas', or my favourite: 'We never send authors to Florida. Nobody reads in Florida'. The readerist publisher, who only wants a bestseller for the sake of funding his poetry list, sees your typical reader with an IQ of 85 dragging his knuckles on the ground. He votes with the man who said nobody ever lost money underestimating public intelligence, and he can't really explain how anyone gets through a 700-page novel. This deep contempt for the audience makes readerism a condition which is fatal to business as well as writing.

A hallmark of readerist attitudes is chasing the market. Readerists are reactive, not proactive. They lack a sense of the integrity of their writing. The book is, in its narrowest meaning, a *product* to them and its value is determined only by market forces. They are always trying to adapt the product to their conception of the market, so they prefer to publish hack writers and clone lists rather than back a range of authors with clear personal voices. The notion of a writer addressing an audience in the confidence of shared experiences, similar tastes and common values is alien to them. You can't avoid readerists but you can – and must – avoid their way of thinking.

PART
2

THE ART AND CRAFT

CHAPTER 3

The Three Choices

Of all the elements in a story, three must be chosen well if the book is to be a bestseller. The location, the central character and the theme of the story are the three things which determine its success.

THE FIRST CHOICE: LOCATION

The setting of a story is one of its most seductive qualities. People will buy a book because its action takes place in a country they love, a landscape which they know or a social environment which they find fascinating. They'll say: 'I bought your book because it was set in television and I'll read anything about television,' or, 'I loved your book because it was set in Africa and I've always wanted to travel in Africa.'

The reader will enjoy the world of a book like a tourist, but the writer must choose that world for one reason only – as the best setting for the theme of the story. Instinct can draw you to a certain time or place, but if your theme is not positively enlarged by that setting it will be nothing but a distracting irrelevance.

The setting of your book is also one of the most important choices you will make affecting its attractiveness to a publisher and ultimate commercial success. Publishers have a strong herd instinct: when John Grisham had a huge hit with a legal thriller, the law suddenly became hot, sexy and fashionable and publishers fell over themselves to produce copycat legal stories. Many of them didn't understand why the law got hot in the first place. An author can't afford such ignorance. If you decide to follow a location trend, or accept such a suggestion from a publisher, you will need to understand, instinctively or analytically, what it is about that arena that has made it significant.

A satisfying book has a very strong sense of location, which derives from much more than mere geography. Whatever place, time or subculture the author chooses, whatever aspiration the author has towards documentary realism, for the reader the setting of the book must be a magic ground, a place of dreams and images whose events can be read metaphorically. Readers will enter this world knowing that it is a fiction, but at the same time needing a powerful sense of its reality to satisfy their critical intelligence. They need certainty about the physical surroundings of the action, so that they can imagine them in atmosphere or detail, and beyond that, they need also to be sure of the unseen features of this world, its ideals, values and morals, and to know where the author stands in relation to that invisible landscape.

The Magic Ground

Every reader begins a book expecting the author to hold out her hand and lead him away – somewhere. Anywhere. Anywhere but where he is now. The magic ground of a story is anywhere which is not the reader's own world, because the reader needs to get outside that world in order to be able to make sense of it.

Creating the magic ground is like beginning a fairy tale: 'Once upon a time, long ago, in a kingdom far away . . .' It means giving your readers the signs they are waiting for, the signs which will allow them to enter the story as an emotional experience, to relax their critical judgement and surrender to the spell of your writing. 'Once upon a time' is a phrase which triggers instant relaxation. If you say those words with authority to a group of bright, well-educated adults you will be able to watch them lean back, smiling, stress visibly draining away as they anticipate the story that is to come.

Star Wars (the novel) begins simply, 'Another galaxy, another time.' All stories take place at a distinct remove from daily life; science fiction writers have it easy because the primary definition of their genre is that the story is placed in the fantasy future. For most authors, the challenge is to create their parallel universe within contemporary reality.

Like the ancient worlds of gods and heroes, which were described as being in the sky, on a mountaintop or beneath the sea, the realm of the story is just over the reader's horizon, just outside the reader's experience, but not beyond the reader's imagination. It is often an aspirational setting, inhabited by people who are perceived as important because they are exceptionally clever, skilled, courageous, powerful, evil, attractive or wealthy – individuals whose actions can have immense impact on the everyday human world.

The world of the story can be full of abundant blessings; the benefits which in real life can only be attained with difficulty and struggle (if at all) are part of the environment here. It can also be a world of extraordinary evil, where extremes of degradation and deprivation exist, where adversaries also have superhuman powers. They threaten the protagonist with tragedy, personal ruin or death; they may threaten humanity itself with disaster on an apocalyptic scale.

Despite its exceptional qualities, the world of the story also needs to have every aspect of familiarity – human dilemmas and dimensions, recognisable people and convincing detail. A very common mistake made by would-be bestseller writers is the choice of an exotic setting which they find immensely attractive, but have no experience of and cannot create with confidence. The old advice to 'write about what you know' is sound, because the universal can be found in your own known world. If you want to use an environment which you don't know, you must research it until, in the words of screen writer and lecturer Robert McKee, 'you know your world as God knows this one.' I would advise a writer who *thinks* she knows the environment of her story to research it as if she knew nothing, because there is a great difference between a casual familiarity with a place and knowing it intimately enough to be able to call up from memory every detail you need to write about it.

At the very start of the book, the writer must give the reader the sign he is looking for, the confirmation that this is a magic ground. In the most compelling stories this is done in the first paragraph, and certainly within the first two pages of the book. This sign is any clear indication of this world's supernatural dimensions – of the dangers, powers and emotions which will come into play later.

One of the most famous descriptions in popular fiction is the beginning of Daphne du Maurier's *Rebecca*. The heroine is literally in a dream: 'Last night I dreamt I went to Manderley again.' In the nightmarish picture which follows the reader is immediately informed that this is a realm of high tragedy. Du Maurier was a master of sinister beginnings, and these two paragraphs not only set the scene of the drama, but also indicate the metaphorical arc of the story and compel the reader to discover its mystery.

The description is of the drive leading to the mansion of which the heroine became mistress when she married its owner, where she struggled against and finally vanquished the memory of his bewitching first wife. The mystery of what trauma prompted the heroine's dream and how the estate's desolation came about is immediately fascinating. Trees overhanging the drive make it a terrifying dark tunnel, and her journey down it is symbolic of her own fearful rebirth.

> It seemed to me I stood by the iron gate leading to the drive, and for a while I could not enter, for the way was barred to me. There was a padlock and a chain upon the gate. I called in my dream to the lodge-keeper, and had no answer, and peering closer through the rusted spokes of the gate I saw that the lodge was uninhabited.
>
> No smoke came from the chimney, and the little lattice

windows gaped forlorn. Then, like all dreamers, I was possessed of a sudden with supernatural powers and passed like a spirit through the barrier before me. The drive wound away in front of me, twisting and turning as it had always done ... Nature had come into her own again and little by little, in her stealthy insidious way, had encroached upon the drive with long, tenacious fingers. The woods, always a menace even in the past, had triumphed in the end. They crowded, dark and uncontrolled, to the borders of the drive. The beeches with white, naked limbs leant close to one another, their branches intermingled in a strange embrace, making a vault above my head like the archway of a church. And there were other trees as well, trees that I did not recognize, squat oaks and tortured elms that straggled cheek by jowl with the beeches, and had thrust themselves out of the quiet earth, along with monster shrubs and plants, none of which I remembered.

The Real Place

The beginning of *Rebecca* is a long descriptive passage by modern standards, and later writers made their messages bolder and more economical. At the start of *The Day of the Jackal* Frederick Forsyth gives his readers a much more concise invitation to the magic ground:

> It is cold at six-forty in the morning of a March day in Paris, and seems even colder when a man is about to be executed by firing squad.

Forsyth, a former television foreign-news reporter, used factual detail with immense authority. The documentary style he developed is now widespread. It imposes a dry precision on a book and suits stories of action more than those of emotion. Particularly in placing the story, a few telling facts, used with skill, are much more powerful than a large tract of fascinating research which nonetheless impedes the narrative.

Forsyth has a sure instinct for necessary and unnecessary information: in the rest of his first page he swiftly creates a sense of place with the distant noise of traffic from the city centre, the colour of the gravel and the pigeons startled by the gunfire, without lingering for a wide shot of the prison yard, let alone the colour of the firing squad's uniforms.

The Time

A story is always about here and now, whatever the period in which it is set. In time, the author has five choices: the eternal present, the present, the future, the recent past and the historical past.

It is common for the precise era of a bestselling book to be undefined – some, like Fay Weldon's *Life and Loves of a She-Devil* – are also set in places which are never identified. A story may seem more powerful if it takes place in the eternal present, because its mythical nature is emphasised and the universality of its theme can emerge more clearly. The characters have a small stage and the action is confined in a narrow frame. The ideas are extremely accessible – if the action is current and the year unspecified, readers will assume that the story is happening at the time they are reading.

In the eternal present, most of the world outside the story has to be excluded, so the reader never discovers which political party is in power or which TV show is top of the ratings, although a recurring external event – like conflict in the Middle East or Elizabeth Taylor's marriages – can make an appearance. Care needs to be taken with ephemeral everyday details like clothes, cars, music and brand names because they can anchor the time intrusively.

In the eternal present a story feels more intense, even to the point of claustrophobia. Emotional themes gain strength from this treatment, and the author is free to create without being concerned about anachronisms or accuracy in period detail.

The present is a more difficult choice. It's exciting to capture the moment, and novels which succeed in defining their own time can become hugely fashionable, but a book may take months or years to finish and as much time again or more to find a publisher, by which time the original, brilliant contemporary references will seem tired. Allowing another year for publication, another year before the paperback appears and, if it is backlisted, five years of shelf life in addition, they will be meaningless.

Right now is also a hard time to get in focus. You need to be confident that what you are choosing to define the present will be what still defines it in five or ten years' time, and you need to consider that what defines the present for you must also define it for your readers. So your country had a recession this year – but what about the rest of the world?

Great novels of their age tend to be first novels, and the authors seem to have exceptional difficulty in consolidating their success with second books. If you are confident that you are as far ahead of your time as Scott Fitzgerald, that you can write as fast and be published as quickly – and keep your life on the rails afterward – then your book *may* be the great novel of its age. Remember that acute social observation is dazzling, but not a substitute for sound construction. If you are in doubt, let go of the more perishable references in the story.

The only reason for a book to be set either in the past or in the future is that it allows the present to be addressed more effectively. The future automatically classifies your story as science fiction, but a story set in the future must relate to the present. Science fiction is a flourishing genre from which very few books become bestsellers. The ones that do are exceptionally successful because they rehearse our huge and vivid fears about the future of the world – although increasingly the most notable science fiction novels are in fact set in the eternal present, making the threat of knowledge without morality absolutely immediate.

Shifting an anxiety into the future allows it to attain huge proportions. In *Jurassic Park* two widespread fears – about the morality of both genetic engineering and mass tourism – appear as big as the tyrannosaurus and threaten the world. The future alone, much as its devotees enjoy imagining it, does not make a story. Science fiction which is dramatically sound but does not exercise and finally allay a fear we have about the future will only appeal to sci-fi readers, not to a mainstream audience.

Readers of science fiction are also perhaps the most critical of all, and the easiest to lose if the details of the fantasy are inadequate. When well-achieved, however, such details can make a science-fiction scenario absolutely irresistible.

The recent past is another favoured setting in popular fiction. The events of recent history are known and the images familiar. Much of the audience can take nostalgic pleasure in the setting, although they can equally well be alienated by anachronisms.

A traumatic event, especially war, will remain a powerful setting for years, and perhaps decades, afterwards while the emotional dust settles and we gather reassurance that life will go on. Two of the books discussed in detail here are set in World War II, and one in a fictional aftermath period. The recent past can provide an intensity which the present may seem to lack.

Correcting history is a particular reason for locating a story in the recent past. History very quickly becomes less a question of fact than of belief, and your readers will have a set of prevailing beliefs about what happened in the recent past, which you may set out to overturn in your book by exposing a real-life fraud or whitewash. Such books can be hugely successful, but their timing is crucial. People are not always ready to hear that they were wrong, that their gods had feet of clay. *A Bridge Too Far*, the film about a disastrous action towards the end of World War II, was made in 1977; had such a film about a tragic defeat for the Allies been made in 1947, it would have found no audience.

When the time for your idea is coming, there will be clues in the culture − legal action pending, concern expressed by insiders in memoirs, speeches or specialist publications. Watch for these signs. Sociologists have their own concept of critical mass: when around 15% of the population holds a belief, it is only a matter of time before it becomes a majority opinion. If you intend to challenge a widely held view of recent history, you will be most successful if that critical mass of opinion already exists to support you. Your book will then become part of the landslide process of social change.

Recent events can be so traumatic that a writer can only address them acceptably by portraying something analogous that happened years earlier. The year 1970 saw the release of two films about the insanity of war, *M*A*S*H*, set in the Korean war of the 1950s, and *CATCH–22*, from Joseph Heller's novel, set during World War II. Both were direct comments on the Vietnam war, which ended in 1972, but so traumatised America that films addressing it realistically did not appear until the late Eighties.

An author writing a book set in the past will need to work with time-lines to be aware of the events which impinge on the story – your hero would have been very lucky to catch a bus in London in the first week of May 1925, for example; it was the first week of the General Strike. Chronological facts alone are not always enough, either. Readers will have notions of what did or didn't happen at a certain time. In a Catherine Cookson story I encountered a barbed-wire fence on a farm in 1895. It seemed so unlikely that I looked it up, and found that the use of barbed wire *would* have been possible at that time. Nevertheless, it clashed with my picture of Victorian husbandry. And as well as events, the attitudes of the past need to be remembered: was it hard to get a job? How guilty would a couple feel about having sex before marriage? How did children speak to their parents?

The historical past poses problems. I am a writer who loves recreating daily life in a distant time down to the smallest charming detail, and in Europe such passages in my books have been heaped with praise, but I have watched American editors skim them with glazed eyes. Europeans, living with the institutions, buildings, art and landscapes of their ancestors, experience the past as a natural context to the present, but American culture is founded on the rejection of everything that has gone before. To Americans, the past is worse than boring, it is alien. A writer interested in an American audience should be aware that most American publishers consider history the kiss of death. Even a few paragraphs of background to a modern story will have an editor's pencil poised.

Certain periods in the past offer the writer an extreme social climate which can add great power to a story's theme. The classic romantic novel, which is concerned with an initially powerless heroine struggling for control of her life, suits the Victorian era particularly well since society was then at a nadir of oppressive sexism. Stories which address racism likewise gain from a colonial setting.

Where You Stand

A location is more than a place. It is also a moral climate, and this too is something which the author needs to define at the start of the book's development. The characters will operate in this moral atmosphere and challenge the values imposed by their environment. It is important for the reader to know as early as possible what is considered right and wrong in this place, what is admired and what is not. Most bestsellers give this information early, which also gives it weight, so when the protagonist fights the system it will be a powerful adversary.

The opening line of *Pride and Prejudice*, 'It is a truth universally acknowledged that a single man in possession of a good fortune must be in want of a wife,' immediately takes the reader into the marriage-mad, materialistic world against which both hero and heroine will hold out to the end. Not every author wants to adopt the tone of lofty irony in which Jane Austen chronicled the foolishness of the nineteenth-century drawing room. The same sort of information can be tucked into a simple description:

The whole of Changi hated the King. They hated him for his muscular body, the clear glow in his blue eyes. In this twilight world of the half alive there were no fat or well-built or round or smooth or fair-built or thick-built men. There were only faces dominated by eyes and set on bodies that were skin

> over sinews over bones. No difference between them but age and face and height. And in all this world, only the King ate like a man, smoked like a man, slept like a man, dreamed like a man and looked like a man.

This is from James Clavell's first novel, *King Rat*, set during World War II in a Japanese prison camp in Singapore, where starvation and brutality destroyed normal human values, where honour was a fatal affliction from which the King, a petty criminal, would never suffer.

The reassurance that human nature is not fundamentally evil, that love can conquer death, that women and men are not enemies, that the wicked will ultimately fail and the good triumph after adversity, is what the reader seeks in a story, and may in fact be consciously expecting.

To accept this reassurance from you as the author, the reader needs to know where you stand. You must demonstrate your moral authority, make it clear that you share your readers' notions of what good and evil are, of what is right and wrong, what is trivial and what important. The author can be in advance of developments in the moral consensus of the readers, but not fundamentally at variance with it.

A story in which the author's moral axis is not aligned with that of the readers seems either offensive or pointless. I was once sent a review copy of a novel by a famous actor, a love story in which a husband wanted to win back his estranged wife. Page after page, chapter after chapter, he yearned for her desperately; she had left him because of something he had done, something which was not revealed until the end of the book. In the meantime he made much of his shock at being so lightly deserted. My instinct was that whatever he'd done was actually pretty bad. Finally it was explained that his pregnant wife had walked into their bedroom and found her husband making love to another woman. At this point the protagonist lost my sympathy completely. When published, the book sank without trace despite the author's high publicity profile.

The readers will readily follow the author into a bad world as long as she gains their trust by making her own position clear. This of course allows the reader to experience the full glamour of wickedness without feeling tainted:

> The scent and smoke and sweat of a casino are nauseating at three in the morning. Then the soul-erosion produced by high gambling – a compost of greed and fear and nervous tension – becomes unbearable and the senses awake and revolt from it.
>
> James Bond suddenly knew that he was tired . . .
>
> CASINO ROYALE
> *Ian Fleming*

This was the public's first introduction to Bond, a hero always able to walk out of hellfire unscathed. In life, Ian Fleming, like his hero, loved gambling and spent time in casinos, but here he took pains to present the green-baize tables with the disgust that readers in the Fifties considered appropriate.

The Bond thrillers were the first to appeal because of their aspirational setting, although the ratio of fast cars, beautiful lovers, large guns, Savile Row suits and bottles of vintage Veuve Cliquot is much lower in the books than the later films suggest. Aspirational backgrounds offend the reader if they are crassly presented as desirable for their own sake. Readers will feel hostility and suspicion, whether or not they envy the life in the story's gilded world. Writers who use these locations with success emphasise their own moral discrimination and never suggest that characters are rich, powerful or privileged without at the same time indicating whether they deserve what they've got. In Jackie Collins' *Hollywood Wives*, it takes one word only:

> Elaine Conti awoke in her luxurious bed in her luxurious Beverly Hills mansion, pressed a button to open the electrically controlled drapes, and was confronted by the sight of a young man clad in a white T-shirt and dirty jeans pissing a perfect arc into her mosaic tiled swimming pool.

'Luxurious' once would have said nothing; 'luxurious' twice says spoiled bitch. Collins uses humour to detach herself from

Hollywood and all its works, and is always on the side of the reader, ridiculing the antics of her supposedly glamorous characters. Their world is often threatened by an outcast, a nemesis from the underclass, an avenger from the real world, whose vengeance permanently anchors the moral axis of the story to that of the reader.

THE SECOND CHOICE: CENTRAL CHARACTER

The central character of a bestseller must be two things in one: a real person and an archetype.

As a person, the central character is so recognisable that the truth of the story is beyond doubt. As an archetype, the central character carries the reader into the emotional experience of the story and opens up her unconscious mind. The reader identifies with the character and can feel the whole story as if it is happening to *her*, in this way being emotionally imprinted with the experience and absorbing its lessons unconsciously. The story itself becomes a ritual in which the battles of life are acted out. It is a process which Jung called the 'participation mystique'; to Freud it was 'projective identification'.

Creating a character who can fulfil this archetypal function is not a matter of matching them to any kind of pattern, or awarding them ideal qualities. A reader should feel a sense of recognition when the hero appears, because the two need to share values and experiences, but the idea that popular fiction characters are stereotypes, all created out of the same moulds, is false. A stereotypical figure is the product of a writer with a basic disrespect for his readers, and can never engage the reader emotionally.

In most popular fiction there is one central character and one main narrative line, but when a story begins to develop in your imagination there may be a group of people in it, all equally intriguing, from whom one will later emerge to take the centre stage. In a few stories there are two central characters and two entwining narrative lines: those two characters need to represent a duality, to have opposing attitudes or traits. If one is active, the other needs to be passive; if one is conformist the other must be rebellious. My first novel was about two sisters, one who accepted her grandmother's ideas of femininity and married young, the other who rejected them, ran away from home and became a singer.

Rarely, a story develops as an ensemble piece, with a group of central characters and a mesh of plot lines. This is much more common in women's novels; in fact, all the great multi-protagonist stories – *Grand Hotel* by Vicki Baum, *The Group* by Mary McCarthy, *The Joy Luck Club* by Amy Tan and Jackie Collins' *Hollywood* series – have been written by women. In discussing the difference between the sexes, the communications specialist Joe Tannenbaum[1] notes that women have a 'diffused' ego orientation and an 'inclusive' concept of reality which may enable them to identify successfully with more than one person, while a man's ego orientation is 'exclusive' and disposes him to see all reality in relation to himself.

From the technical point of view, multi-protagonist stories are pure hell to write. They offer the reader a broader and richer picture than a simple narrative and spread the risk that the reader won't like the central character, but for a male reader in particular a multi-protagonist story may offer too many choices, so instead of identifying with one character, or one character at a time, he will feel uninvolved and never really get into the story.

Playing God

Making people is not easy. It is difficult to define any character when you begin thinking of a book, because character and plot are indivisible. How the hero reacts to a challenge is as important as what the challenge is in determining what happens next. It is often not until you begin to work out the synopsis of your book that you can define the central character.

---

[1] *Male & Female Realities* by Joe Tannenbaum, Robert Erdmann Publishing, 1989. pp77, 85.

It may not seem like this at the start, but you know your central character very well. Creating them in writing is a matter of trusting your knowledge, of discovering the person rather than making them up. For many writers it is the most instinctive part of the process. The slightest sketch of a plot will contain within it the germ of the protagonist, who will become a fully rounded human being as the story develops. Like a new-born baby, that germ is perfect in every detail and all you have to do is nurture it.

Many books start with a character. What anchors the writer's attention may be a few words of overheard conversation, the way a friend keeps smiling as she screws her life up, the look in the eyes of a face in a photograph. Occasionally an entire person will simply walk out of your imagination, so fully realised that you know them as well as your oldest friend and never hesitate in deciding what they will do or say.

More commonly, only one quality of the protagonist's character will be clear at the outset. Many writers then build up a character by the Frankenstein method, stitching together several attributes of people they know in life; the result may be able to walk and talk but it may not be able to tap-dance. The creature will be more graceful if you allow it to evolve from your imagination. Some writers go in for outright body-snatching, putting a whole known person in their story. This is no problem with minor characters, but you may find that you only want the truth that fits, that you need your central character to do things which the real model would never do.

Abstract or philosophical thinkers may begin with the theme of the book and develop a character to act it out, and those whose technique is very objective may start with an event in the plot. Working this way, from structure to character, can still create a rounded, credible person.

By the time you are happy with your scenario and have written a synopsis, you should also know your protagonist well enough to be able to write the key elements of their character down on a card, add a picture to it and pin the card up over your desk to be used to keep them acting in character as the story grows. This technique is discussed in more detail in

Chapter 5 (*see* p87). If the protagonist keeps falling out of character, you may have grown attached to a personality which is incapable of acting in such a way as to make your story happen. In this case you will need either to redraw the character or rebuild the plot.

The Seven Questions

That one quality with which the protagonist first appears is the foundation of their character, their cardinal quality. It is an extreme trait which is both their curse and their blessing. They may be curious, angry, loving, honest, rebellious, conventional, revengeful, fair-minded, or any of an almost infinite number of other qualities.

There are two approaches to raising a real person on this foundation, and no reason not to use both of them. One is the instinctive method: you work like an actor and become the person, feeling their emotions and sensing their behaviour. Imagining yourself inside the character, you look outwards through their eyes and react to the events of the story, discovering how they feel and what they are going to do. You find yourself speaking their lines and adopting their body language. Experiential research – going off and doing some of the things that your protagonist will do – can help this process.

The other approach is analytical. There are probably as many ways of breaking down a personality as there are different individuals in the world, but one I would recommend is to answer seven questions:

1) What is the cardinal quality?

2) What opposes that? This is the trait which is holding the hero back at the start of the story, the inner enemy which they have to overcome. Hamlet is vengeful but indecisive. Shirley Valentine is adventurous, but feels she doesn't deserve her dreams. Very often, especially in women protagonists, the opposing quality is some kind of fear.

The tension between the cardinal quality and the opposing

quality is what creates light and shade and makes the character real. The balance usually tips towards the better quality in moral terms, but there can be no once-and-for-all victory. A protagonist with no opposing quality is two-dimensional.

3) What do they want? At the start of the story, the hero will have a goal, dream or ambition, even if it is just to have a quiet life and die with his boots on. Quite often it is a mistaken aim, framed by the opposing quality, and replaced by something more admirable as the story unfolds.

4) What is behind them? The background to the character, their family, education and past experiences, the influences which have shaped them before the start of the story. Some writers research and define this so minutely that they can show you the house where the protagonist was born and draw up their horoscope as well.

5) What is above them? Their higher self, their morality, their beliefs, the values which they have perhaps forgotten or not yet learned, which will become the ethical basis for their actions. This is something which will be revealed as the story continues, and be tested by its events.

6) What is below them? This is their worst nightmare, their deepest fear, the depth to which they will sink before the last battle. It is what they become when they are very afraid, when their higher self is out of sight.

7) Where will they end? The final definition: how the protagonist will change, who they will be at the end of the journey. The hero's quest is for himself; when he succeeds he will have integrated the cardinal and opposing traits of his character and achieved a higher level of maturity.

There is no rule demanding that the character of the protagonist should change in the course of a story, but if it doesn't, if he learns nothing or refuses his challenges, he will have failed and the audience will be outraged if you reward him with a happy ending. This is a major difference between a novel and film or television, in which the inner lives of the characters are much less visible and the time-span relatively condensed.

Answering these seven questions will define the deep character of your protagonist, from which you will be able to draw all the superficial details of characterisation, idiosyncrasies, tastes and choices. Are they tidy? Can they cook? Do they wear jeans and if so how old and what colour? What do they say when they answer the telephone? When a fictional person seems real, all these small things reinforce the core character. Spray-painting random eccentricities on a flat figure will not bring it to life.

Good, Bad and Scarlett

Notice that in analysing the core character above, I have not divided qualities into good or bad, positive or negative. It is not helpful to start classifying a character in those terms, reducing your story to a morality play and losing all the tension and ambiguity which make a human personality.

Consider Scarlett O'Hara, the heroine of *Gone With The Wind*. Her cardinal quality is courage and her selfishness opposes it. She wants her own way, especially in the matter of marrying Ashley Wilkes. Behind her is the Old South and her mother's notions of honour and ladylike conduct. Above her is her best self, a truly heroic woman who can sacrifice herself and save lives, even the life of Ashley's wife. At her worst, she's a callous grasping bitch who steals her sister's man, causes his death and can't love her own child. At the end, although she changed when the Old South died, although she took up all the early challenges of her journey and won, she refuses the last fight. She will not love Rhett. She does not change until it is too late for him, and the end is tragic.

Archetypal Architecture

Scarlett is not a good person; she can do good, but from selfish motives. She isn't nice and the author does not approve of her.

Nevertheless, generations of readers have loved her and wanted her to have her final victory. She loses everything, she suffers, she is courageous and she never gives up. Much of her wickedness seems forgivable because nothing has prepared her for the trials of her life.

Having played God with reasonable success and created a real person, you need to ask yourself if your creation can inspire that kind of loyalty. The readers are on your side here, they begin the book expecting and searching for the one character they will identify with, through whom they will experience everything that happens. Much of the writer's task is not to hamper this process.

There are widespread misconceptions about what makes a character sympathetic. The very word is misleading: empathetic would be more accurate. An empathetic character is one into which you can project yourself. A sympathetic character is one who appears likeable, and they are significantly different. A likeable character will probably be a nice person with many admirable qualities. Yawn, yawn. How do you feel when you meet real people like that? They can be rather awesome in their goodness, so perfect that you feel like an inadequate worm around them. And they don't have much fun in life. They have even less fun in books, because wholly likeable characters are desperately hard to write. Sweat all you can over them, they come out screamingly dull. Think of Melanie Wilkes.

In getting an idea of what makes a character empathetic, think of the way you feel about a lover or a friend. Yes, you think they're brilliant, you love all the good things about them – energy, wit, warmth, their ability to start your car in the snow, whatever. What actually bonds you to them is what you share, all the things you agree about, your common view of the world. And the moments when they make you melt are their moments of weakness, when they put salt in their coffee because they're stressed or when they cry over *Dumbo*. They certainly aren't perfect and sometimes they drive you crazy, but if anyone attacks them you will leap to their defence. Similarly, a character with whom the reader can identify will not be perfect and will sometimes drive everyone crazy. There will be good in them, they will have the ability to do great things, but not all the time.

Common Ground

Clearly, it is not possible to create a character with whom millions of people can share all their opinions. The shared morality of the readers and the central character will be the simplest and most basic of ideals like love, truth, justice, equality and the survival of humanity. At heart, the central character wants to help make the world go round. On first meeting that may not be at all obvious, in which case there should be a hint that they *could* do the right thing, if given the right encouragement.

As the story progresses, the central character may do things which are bad, especially at their lowest point when their old way of life is challenged. In order not to disrupt the readers' identification, the reason must be clear – they were forced, they were deceived, they were misguided. Guilt, regret and willingness to reform are then in order, and if they do not express these then retribution must follow.

Readers will be violently alienated if the central character wilfully does something immoral and gets away with it, but every book has a different moral climate. Cold-blooded killing is acceptable in a thriller but in an adolescent love story kicking a dog can be a crime. Rape and cruelty to children are never right, and unless you are examining the issues in your story it is advisable to keep your protagonist out of moral minefields like abortion, blood sports and sexual harassment.

As well as sharing the reader's feelings about the biggest issues in life, an empathetic character feels the same about some of the little things. They hate automated telephone queuing systems, tailgating truck drivers and snobby waiters. They worry that too much cola will rot their teeth or that there's unnoticed baby sick on their best power suit. They envy roller-bladers and people who can play the piano. These tiny touches need no more than a line and are best used sparingly, although Raymond

Chandler gave Philip Marlowe an attitude on almost everyone he met.

Vulnerability

The hero figure in a fairy tale is usually the youngest sister, the smallest animal, the orphan child, the widow's son, or an outcast in the community. Automatically, they have the audience's sympathy. Similarly, throughout popular culture, the protagonists are often in some way disadvantaged. They can be lonely or unhappy, set apart from their peers because of their race, sex or background. If they start off near the top of the heap, they lose everything. It is the central character's vulnerability which endears them to the reader more than anything else, but the reader is well accustomed to clumsy grabs for sympathy and will view stereotypical ragged orphans with cynicism.

A very powerful way to demonstrate your character's vulnerability is to make it their Achilles heel, a little weakness in their character, something normal which is not a problem most of the time but could just destroy everything. Maybe they're a little too gullible, or careless or unassertive.

In the film *Alien*, Sigourney Weaver's Achilles heel is her kindness, a very significant flaw since the story, made in 1979, sets out to prove that a woman can also save the world. Out in deep space in a rusting hulk of a ship, androgynous in overalls, tougher and smarter than all the men around her, she is still soft enough to talk to the ship's cat. At the climax of the film the monster has killed all the rest of the crew and is now looking for her. She programmes the ship to blow up and begins a desperate run for the shuttle craft, escaping through the half-wrecked corridors, rocked by explosions, expecting to run into the creature's hideous jaws round every corner. I first saw this film in a packed cinema in Los Angeles and by this point the audience was hysterical. Then she stops to catch the cat, put it in its carrying basket and take it with her. The audience went crazy. Half of them jumped to their feet yelling, 'DON'T

TAKE THE CAT!' It was participation mystique on the scale of grand opera. That's what vulnerability can do for you.

The rest of the cast will develop in relation to the central character, with opposite or offsetting qualities which will create friction and bring the protagonist into sharper focus. Chapter Eight (*see* p160) deals with the creation of the supporting characters.

You will discover – usually long after the book is finished – that the central character is an aspect of yourself, that their struggle between cardinal and opposing qualities is your own struggle writ large. It is no help at all to figure this out at the start of the book, but it does explain why you know this character so well, and why you are so strongly drawn to their story.

THE THIRD CHOICE:
THEME

Whatever the writer's intention, every story has a theme, a controlling idea, a moral, a proposition which is proved in its action, a conclusion which can be drawn from its end, something which it 'goes to show'.

Nobody worries if a pop song is simple, direct and didactic, but if readers catch a book telling them what to think, they won't like it. A story is experienced emotionally, not intellectually. Understanding a book's theme is not a conscious process. A reader opens a book wanting satisfying emotional experiences, not a lecture. Even the most cerebral of your readers, who may claim they read for ideas, debate or literary merit, will be seeking the comfort of feeling their anxieties exercised and the pleasure of beautiful language when they open a book.

The theme of a book is the third key factor in its success, but it must be invisible. Much of popular culture is called escapist, but there is really no such thing as escapism, only anxieties which are so terrifying that people cannot contemplate them directly; in a story, these anxieties are metaphorically exercised. If the writer makes the process clear, the reader is forced to confront the terror head on and will choose to escape in another way – by putting down the book.

The theme is the last thing a writer needs to think about. It will be one of your own wishes or beliefs and it will inform your imagination without any conscious effort on your part. Episodes which confirm the theme will seem attractive to you, and you just won't like things which clash with it. Unless you see your book as a work of conscious social engineering, avoid defining your theme too early. Let the story grow until its outline is complete, then look at it and see what it is trying to prove. Books which expound their themes with the utmost rigour and elegance have been written entirely by instinct.

Defining the theme of the story in its initial stages will help the writer to express it as powerfully as possible. The idea will be explored and tested in the events of the plot, and finally demonstrated in the way the story ends. The interaction between the main characters will illuminate the theme. You may create a strand of narrative which conflicts with it, an image system which emphasises it, or sub-plots which reinforce it, and exclude events which muddy the water, which are irrelevant or weakening to it.

A theme is a refined abstract proposition which defines a deep human wish or addresses a deep human fear. It is *not* the same thing as the vague idea or collection of ideas which are usually presented as what the story is 'about' – growing up, finding identity, letting go of the past, the triumph of the underdog, female solidarity, learning to be a parent, male obsession, accepting old age. A book can deal with any of those topics but they will not constitute its underlying argument.

Themes Ancient and Modern

A book's theme can be as old as the human race itself or something recently generated by a major social shift. The eternal themes answer fears which are dark shadows in the mind thrown up from the unconscious, while contemporary themes tackle more conscious anxieties about the changing world.

Because they are allaying fears, themes are mostly positive, affirmative and optimistic. Negative themes, telling us that a value or behaviour is wrong, generate tragedies. Whatever their provenance, all themes are ultimately about our survival, as individuals and as a race, about what will create or protect our lives, families, communities and the world as far as we know it. They tell us, simply, that life will go on.

Life and Love

At the first level, dealing with life, come all the themes about love. Some of these suggest the virtues necessary to achieve love, a question which is eternal although the answers change. In *Gone With The Wind*, love demands self-sacrifice. In the film *Pretty Woman*, love demands self-esteem. Stories about growing up, those which script editors classify as 'maturational' stories, can also contain this theme, or may look at the earlier questions of how parental conflicts can be resolved or what being a woman or a man really means.

Since love is an inconvenient force liable to arise in anti-social ways, the conflicts between love and duty, and between love and social values, are constant. In *The Bridges of Madison County*, love is worth the suffering that duty demands. *The Age of Innocence*, written by Edith Wharton 72 years earlier, criticised a society which valued duty over love.

In the Family

Themes which express wishes and fears about parents, children and the family are very common in soap operas and TV series, which address the area directly. Often the action is located in a family, as with *The Cosby Show* or *Roseanne*, often it is an overt discussion of new family groups, as with *Frazier*, *Ellen* or *My Two Dads*. Family themes in films are common and usually successful, as with *Baby Boom*, *Look Who's Talking I* and *II*, *Mermaids*, or *Three Men and a Baby*, all of which argue that family love can survive modern life given a little old-fashioned self-sacrifice.

The people most interested in a theme are, of course, people to whose lives it is directly relevant. People negotiating the life passage between marriage and parenthood don't have time on their hands for reading, and what leisure they have they prefer to spend with their children rather than isolated in a book. So it is hardly surprising that family themes are not common in fiction. The only major successes in this area are the *Adrian Mole* books, offering wan assurance that a child can survive modern parenting.

While film and TV address the evolution of the family with enthusiasm, books are still circulating ideas which are almost reactionary. *The Good Mother* suggested that a woman had to choose between sexuality and motherhood, while the books of Barbara Taylor Bradford hark back to the dynastic sagas of the Sixties and Seventies. Books such as *The First Wives' Club* and *The Dieter* reassure readers that no husband is better than a bad husband, an idea which the hot media handled in the Seventies. Single mothers, single fathers and step-families, figures which abounded in the novels of Dickens, are at present rare in modern popular fiction; this area seems ripe for regeneration.

Good and Evil

In contrast, a large proportion of bestsellers express themes related to community or society, affirming the triumph of good over evil. Entire genres are dedicated to this proposition – thrillers, crime, espionage and war stories. Good is usually embodied in the protagonist, whose special qualities stand for those of every individual, and evil is constantly appearing in different forms as the focus of social anxiety shifts. John Grisham's stories are models of this kind: *The Firm* demonstrates that one man of integrity can beat the Mafia; *The Pelican Brief* shows that one woman of intelligence can beat racist corruption.

It is worth noting here that although women protagonists are exceptional in the majority of stories about social survival, they are well established in detective fiction, making this genre one in which an author has opportunities to deal with characters and issues which encounter resistance elsewhere. Agatha Christie's Miss Marple is the only grey-haired heroine in fiction who gets respect for her mind rather than her matriarchal status. Women detectives can do and be things which editors find troubling in the heroines of other genres: they can reject men, drink, swear and engage in bare-knuckle fights against sexism.

Known and Unknown

The survival of the human race, the world or the known universe has inspired many of the most celebrated fantasy novels of the past century. These themes assert the essential goodness of humanity, offering reassurance that we are safe in pushing out the boundaries of knowledge, that we are fit to handle the powers that knowledge gives us. They address one of two deep concerns about modern life: that we have offended nature, and nature wants revenge, or that science without morality will destroy human life.

The lengthy factual preamble to *Jurassic Park* makes an overt appeal to the latter anxiety:

The late twentieth century has witnessed a scientific gold rush of astonishing proportions: the headlong and furious haste to commercialize genetic engineering . . .

Biotechnology promises the greatest revolution in human history . . . but the biotechnology revolution differs in three important respects from past scientific transformations.

First, it is broad-based . . . Second, much of the research is thoughtless or frivolous . . . Third, the work is uncontrolled . . .

But most disturbing is the fact that no watchdogs are found among scientists themselves. It is remarkable that nearly every scientist in genetic research is also engaged in the commerce of biotechnology. There are no detached observers. Everybody has a stake.

Outer World and Inner Life

In all popular culture, themes are very strongly related to the passages of life. Stories about growing up and getting wisdom are those which are the most obvious substitutes for mythology. In ancient times, mythical stories and the rituals which enacted them led people through successive gateways to maturity, preparing them for adolescence, marriage, parenthood, leadership, war and death. This preparation enabled each individual to leave behind the familiar attitudes and attachments of the phase they had outgrown and enter a new life pattern, confident of spiritual guidance, with clear and positive ideas of their new social role.

Modern society offers few such rituals, and those that remain don't work very well; a couple who have a white wedding rarely report that the experience prepared them for marriage. Our path to maturity is lonely and difficult to find, and our spiritual guides have fallen to arguing among themselves. The fears aroused at each stage of life are acute, but they are also the signposts which we need.

In explaining the link between mythology and the unconscious, Joseph Campbell called those fears 'dangerous messengers, because they threaten the fabric of security into which we have built ourselves and our family, fascinating because they carry keys that open the whole realm of desired and feared adventure of the discovery of the self. Destruction of the world that we have built and in which we live, and of ourselves within it; but then a wonderful reconstruction of the bolder, cleaner, more spacious and fully human life.'

In addressing these fears, a book becomes a tool for life, which is what the reader was looking for all along. It is no practical help to the writer to be overly aware of the function of a story while he is writing it, but there are moments in a story's development when the knowledge can be helpful.

A story can fail to thrive. It can refuse to put on weight. It will be shadowy and weak, decorative but lacking something which you can't define, all show and no substance. It will insist on presenting itself as just a story. You may probe it carefully and find nothing in it of any universal significance, and you yourself may lose confidence that you can make the commitment to write a book on this basis. If you consider the story from the point of view of what the central character will learn about the next phase of his or her life, the key to its significance will appear. Sometimes moving the protagonist closer to the start of a new life-passage will turn a sketch into a book.

The theme of a book is for the author to know and then forget while the work is completed. If you trust yourself not to start lecturing your reader, write the theme out as a short, positive sentence and put it somewhere where you can see it as you work.

4

The Endless Quest – Research

'I don't write what I know. My great claim is that everything I write is invented.'

Len Deighton

There are authors for whom facts are wings on the imagination and those for whom facts are like Caterpillar boots weighing down every step. You need to know as much as will allow you to envisage your story freely, without any input from that little internal voice saying, 'Could this really happen?' or, 'Did people really worry about stuff like this in Nebraska in 1935?' How much knowledge that is varies enormously from one person to another.

Research is very much a measure of the writer's confidence. Only the very grand can graduate from the facts-who-needs-them? school, like the extremely famous author who conceived her tenth novel as a homage to Dickens, a teeming chronicle of high times and low life in modern London, a brilliant time-capsule with every social nuance exquisitely captured. In this novel the hero called in at a particular cocktail bar whose utter and absolute fashionableness has never been surpassed, and leaned on the brass bar rail.

Which was fine if you didn't know that the bar rail was

chrome. The design of that bar was famous, it won a shelf of awards and it was all about chrome; any fixture that wasn't chromed was a mirror. The designer's drawings had been bought for the dazzled nation and were on permanent display in the Victoria & Albert Museum. Any sighted person who had ever dipped his lips in a margarita in that bar knew that the rail was chrome.

It didn't matter. The novel was a huge hit, serialised in a leading literary magazine, praised to the skies, sold in pallet-loads. Reviewers raved about the author's adroit observation, her rare understanding, her laser-like eye for detail, her evocative urban landscape. Nobody noticed the brass bar rail except me, and I didn't stop reading in consequence. It was a big fat plonking mistake of the kind authors have nightmares about and it made absolutely no difference to the book, because the writer was satisfied with her level of knowledge and told her story with total confidence.

Not many writers can perform this trick. For most, mistakes are fatal. Ken, a friend of mine from Atlanta, Georgia, immediately abandoned a novel about the Old South when the heroine got married with a wreath of magnolia blossoms in her hair. Magnolia blossoms are about the size of soup bowls. They do not wreath well. Being a Yankee, the writer was on borrowed time with Ken anyway.

Mistakes matter because they break the pact between reader and writer. Your readers need to trust you. You need to appear credible to them. They open a book wanting to get into the story and needing little to convince them of the author's authority. Once they have caught you out, however, their trust will be broken and the sense of betrayal is so strong that they may stop reading, or at best continue in a half-hearted, cynical mood which will prevent them ever re-entering the story.

Your readers are sophisticated; they get the same basic information about the world as you do, 98% of it from television, which offers them video coverage of events in the world of which their grandparents would have been completely ignorant. Formal education is now a twenty-year process – 39% of the readers who took part in this book's survey did not complete full-time education until they were over the age of 21. You must expect many of your readers to have specialist knowledge; your books will be read by doctors, lawyers, pharmacists, archaeologists, atomic physicists – people with a much deeper grasp of their own subject than an author could possibly acquire in the normal course of research.

A publisher from a large international paperback house once told me that lack of credibility is the most common fault in books submitted to them directly. The authors, she said, did not have 'big enough lives' to tell their stories with authority. Although the world of books has aspects of an ivory tower, your prospective agents and publishers will be well educated and, in addition, trained to spot mistakes. They may well dismiss popular fiction readers as stupid, but when they read books themselves they will have the same emotional response to a factual mistake as any other reader. All round, authors need to be absolutely sure of any facts they intend to use.

Fact and fiction have been borrowing each other's glamour all over popular culture. Thrillers are introduced with fake news footage, documentaries are dramatised, historical biographies are packed with novelised incidents. Competing for viewers' attention, television news presents facts in the same form as dramas which are complete fiction. The distinction between actuality and imagination is disappearing. Paradoxically, fiction now does not seem like fiction unless it has the patina of fact.

When to Stop

The scope of your book is the first factor which will frame your research. If you are drawn to an intimate scenario involving a handful of characters, leaving time and place undefined to focus all the readers' attention on the emotional content, only the bare essentials are necessary. You don't want your readers to get cerebral, you want them to *feel*. Information in the text will keep throwing the reader into a rational, intellectual mode which will work against your intentions.

Social realism demands a wider picture, taking in the textures and layers of a whole society. This is the realism of Dickens, Hardy, Balzac, Tolstoy and the rest of the nineteenth-century writers, and of many novelists still. Social realism sets human truth against the canvas of current events. It proposes a series of worlds which fit inside each other like Russian dolls. The smallest is the characters' interior space, their inner lives. Next, their outward, but individual relationships. Outside that, they are part of a family group, a community, a neighbourhood, a profession, an urban tribe, an organisation. Beyond that is their nation, and beyond that their world. Events in the outer layers impinge on the inner, and the outer layers are viewed through their medium. Unless you make a conscious choice to exclude certain layers – many women's novels don't venture beyond the first three – you will need to research the whole context of your action including contemporary world events. Social realism requires the study of books, of other media, of society and of human nature.

We live in an information explosion. It's been going on for some time. We are fact junkies, habituated to knowledge, and withdrawal is distressing. It feels more comfortable to be given the essential facts, and many non-essential but fascinating ones in addition, than to have a scene briefly sketched and be left to imagine the detail. Writers like Michael Crichton, Philip Kerr and Frederick Forsyth offer their readers knowledge enhanced with great precision; these writers do not deal in vague allusions, but in factual detail.

Television has created an audience which enjoys knowledge and feels insecure in ignorance. They need and want to know. The questions every journalist is taught to answer as fast as possible – who, where, when, why and how – shape the expectations which a reader brings to a book. People are ravenously and elaborately curious. They enjoy information for its own sake, they want to travel the world of the book like tourists and in some fiction genres the education factor of a story is a major attraction. Enter documentary realism . . .

There are few less prepossessing places to spend a hot afternoon than Kingston International Airport in Jamaica . . . A cleaner ambled in and, with the exquisite languor of such people throughout the Caribbean, proceeded to sweep very small bits of rubbish hither and thither, occasionally dipping a boneless hand into a bucket to sprinkle water over the dusty cement floor. Through the slatted jalousies a small breeze, reeking of the mangrove swamps, briefly stirred the dead air and then was gone. There were only two other passengers in the 'lounge', Cubans perhaps, with jippa-jappa luggage. A man and a woman. They sat close together against the opposite wall and stared fixedly at him, adding minutely to the oppression of the atmosphere. He got up and went over to the shop. He bought a *Daily Gleaner* and returned to his place. Because of its inconsequence and occasionally bizarre choice of news the *Gleaner* was one of his favourite papers. Almost the whole of that day's front page was taken up with new ganja laws to prevent the consumption, sale and cultivation of this local version of marijuana. The fact that de Gaulle had just sensationally announced his recognition of Red China was boxed well down the page. He read the whole paper – 'country newsbits' and all – with the minute care bred of desperation. His horoscope said: 'CHEER UP! Today will bring a pleasant surprise and the fulfilment of a dear wish. But you must earn your good fortune by watching closely for the golden opportunity when it presents itself and then seizing it with both hands.' Bond smiled grimly. He would be unlikely to get on the scent of Scaramanga on his first evening in Havana.

THE MAN WITH THE GOLDEN GUN, 1965

Ian Fleming was the first writer to use documentary realism in popular fiction, and nobody does it better. The technique involves creating an intense sense of actuality from tiny details. The passage above passes casually over the scene like a panning camera, allowing the reader to enjoy deducing information about the setting, but also about the character of the protagonist: impatient, clever, goal-oriented, worldly but affectionate towards those who aren't, humorous even in a frustrating situation, with a tendency towards cynicism. The James Bond of Fleming's books is a three-dimensional figure constructed entirely from detail, although public imagination only retains the .28 Beretta with the skeleton grip and the vodka martini shaken not stirred.

Writers with a natural passion for detail love this technique, but it needs discipline. All the information in the passage quoted above has a purpose. It supports the fabric of the narrative and the reader's relationship with the hero. Gratuitous information, parked in the text like a trophy put on a mantelpiece, clutters the narrative and bores the reader.

Documentary realism is most effectively achieved by highly observant people writing about worlds they know very well, but good experiential research can compensate. Even if you are writing about a familiar world, it is advisable to check your impressions because memories are tricky and everything changes.

Furnishing Your Mind

A good collection of reference works, which makes a great range of information instantly available, enables a writer to find facts with the minimum disruption of their writing schedule and check out ideas immediately even if the Muse decides to drop round at 4am.

A basic reference library could include:

✔ The best dictionary you can afford, say *The Shorter Oxford English Dictionary* in two volumes

✔ At least one guide to modern English grammar

✔ Slang dictionary

✔ Atlas

✔ Motoring atlas of your own country

✔ A world history, such as *Chronicle of the World* and *Chronicle of the Twentieth Century*

✔ Dictionary of mythology, such as *Brewer's Dictionary of Phrase and Fable*

✔ Dictionary of quotations

✔ The Bible, the authorised or King James version

✔ Complete works of Shakespeare

✔ Anthology of English poetry

✔ Guides to the arts: literature, classical music, pop music, art and architecture, design, cinema

✔ Wildlife guide

✔ Family medical encyclopedia

✔ History of costume or fashion

✔ Legal handbook

An additional major investment, worth making when you can, is a large, multi-volume encyclopedia. It doesn't need to be absolutely up to date, since you can find new editions in your library. CD-Rom encyclopedias are very good value and extremely easy to use.

A thesaurus, which groups thousands of familiar words according to their meaning so the writer can browse in search of an alternative in the event of vocabulary failure, is not essential. Most of them are inadequate, and contain so many archaic words that they are actually unhelpful and can deaden a writer's style.

This is an expensive shopping list. Most writers assemble their libraries slowly, buying the best they can afford at the time, later replacing paperbacks with hardbacks and old with new. Some titles, like the medical encyclopedia, need to be up to date but most reference books can be bought second-hand, or bought at a discount price from a book club or remainder shop. Multi-volume encyclopedias are sometimes sold at auction or through small ads in local newspapers.

The Seven Fields – Structuring Research

Research is fascinating. Research is fun. You meet people, you go places, you sit in strange bars telling the regulars about your book and they are enthralled. You can read with a clear conscience. It certainly beats writing. Most authors love research. For most authors the problem is not how much research to do, but when to stop.

A research schedule will help you make the best use of your available resources – time and money. It will also make sure that you follow each strand of investigation through to the point where you feel that you have a good-enough grasp of it to write without hesitation. The task usually falls into seven fields:

1) Start-up Research: This is what you need to do to put flesh on the bones of your ideas, and to find out if they will work. You need to know that the events which you propose are actually possible. In the start-up phase:

✔ get an overview by reading the books which are standard works for the subjects you need to cover, and start making notes

✔ note from their bibliographies titles for further reading

✔ make time-lines for your story – events in the country where it is located, and events in the rest of the world

✔ get expert advice on crucial points

Expert advice needs to be good – relevant and up to date. You can get it from academics, technical journalists and the leading members of every profession – who are usually highly paid and highly stressed. A telephone call is enough at this stage. Experts can be extraordinarily helpful and generous, or not, but difficult as it is to cold-call the eminent, it is better to approach the highest authority you dare than to be advised wrongly. You might, for instance, if you needed a legal point explained, be able to network your way to the delightful former law tutor of a friend of your cousin – retired five years, not interested in your subject anyway and sadly not much help.

Start-up research commences as soon as your ideas begin to develop. It will enlarge your understanding and prevent you from pouring your energy into an entirely incredible concept. As a researcher, I once had the nasty job of telling an author that there was a problem with the basic premise of his plot, a little point of genetics which any fifteen-year-old biology student would have understood. In addition, another section of the story was located in Istanbul in a specific year. In that year, a military curfew was in force in the city; after 8pm, his characters would have been arrested on the street. I suggested modifying the story accordingly and he decided to ignore my advice. The TV rights had already been sold and the location shooting completed. In the end, the book and the series told totally different stories and neither did much for the author's credibility.

2) Background Research: Once you know that you can proceed:

✔ put together a basic reading list.

Nearly all the books you need for a broad, general understanding can be found in that neighbourhood cornucopia of thought, your public library. As well as factual books, include any major novels dealing with your subjects. You need to compare your treatment of a subject with that of other writers for several reasons: fictional descriptions are often better sources than factual records; an important book will have shaped the general conception of that subject; you may unconsciously duplicate this work and then be accused of plagiarism; your future publisher or agent may be aware of, or even devoted to, this same work and you don't want to look like an idiot; lastly, there is the possibility that when your book is published it may be given to that very same author to review.

✔ begin drafting a budget

Although you may have only the haziest ideas of what you want to spend in the course of researching your book, it is worth estimating your costs at the beginning; major financial decisions will present themselves – like buying a very expensive academic study or downloading a whole thesis through the Internet – and a budget will give you a basis on which to make up your mind. If you want to travel, that will also be a major expense and if it is outside your budget you will need extra time for reading on the location.

✔ decide how much time you can dedicate to research and draw up a schedule for it dividing that time between the main research areas. If you want to use interviews and to travel, get your background reading done first so you have a clear idea of what you need to ask and to see.

✔ as you work through your reading list, note down any specialised books you will need for the next phase and, if you need to order them from private libraries or second-hand dealers, do so now.

✔ decide if you want to consult any newspaper or magazine archives, find out where they are held and what your costs will be. Public libraries keep newspaper files; magazines are usually held by their publishers. Both are also kept in national libraries.

✔ sample the technical and specialist magazines in a good newsagent. These can be an extremely fruitful resource and it can be worth placing an order for a few months.

✔ take a good TV guide and tape any useful television programmes. Video records are extremely useful because they capture every nuance of a situation, from the body language and tone of voice to the cloud formations overhead. If you miss the programme, find out from the producer's office if there is a transcript available.

✔ buy the books you know you will need to keep on your desk.

✔ talk to people about what you're doing. People love helping authors. You will be given advice, loaned books, introduced to dozens of third parties and bored to near-death – but some of it will be very useful.

3) Specialised Research: This will take you deep into your subject and will usually involve publications which are not easy to find. Finding technical data is straightforward, but the kind of information that is pure gold to a writer can often be found by browsing through very minor books – personal memoirs, tedious oral histories, collections of letters and bad novels. The writers in journals as inconsequential as school magazines, regimental newsletters, local newspapers, PTA cookbooks or fan-club circulars have wonderful, authentic voices which will add texture to your characterisation.

There is little point in working from a reading list now, because you will be feeling your way. To trace the publications you want, search the public library and bookshop stock lists first. Then, if you have to, proceed to the national library, or a large private institution like the London Library, both of which have membership requirements and fees. University libraries, most of which can be used by the public for a small charge, keep not only books but the theses of their graduates.

Specialist libraries are kept by an extraordinary range of bodies – charities, political lobbies, professional associations, local-history societies, religious foundations and government departments. Organisations employing barely twenty people can still have libraries which are treasure troves. When you come across an organisation connected with the field you are researching, ask if they have a library.

If you have time, browse remainder shops, charity shops and second-hand book shops for useful volumes at bargain prices. Books which have gone out of print can also be bought through specialist dealers. Their method is not particularly elaborate – they usually just advertise in book-dealers' magazines and you could profitably do the same yourself; you will almost certainly be offered an undreamt-of range of related publications as well.

This phase will take in press archive research. There may be a choice between bound copies, microfiche, database or CD-Rom, of which the last two are much the most efficient. You will get the best out of the others if you know exactly which dates you want to look up. Microfiche, a miniature plastic slide of every page of a newspaper, is simple to use but fiddly, and seldom indexed. You need patience. Microfiche and bound copies are useful if you want a general feel for the events of a period and to give you the style of news reports or features in the past.

Most archives offer photocopying, or a print-out from the database, at a small charge. Some newspapers also produce yearbooks and you may be able to find copies of these through second-hand or out-of-print booksellers.

4) Interviews: As long as your interviewee is articulate, a conversation can be the best way of investigating the quality of an experience you cannot have yourself. The technique is not mysterious, and the main problem is getting through the door. It is best to approach interviewees through someone you both know, but do not be reluctant to approach a stranger. Nobody ever died of rejection.

✔ begin with a telephone call (unless your introducer specifically asks you to write a letter)

Give your name, explain that you are researching a novel and if you have a publisher give their name as well. Explain what kind of information you want and, if they agree to talk to you, pick a convenient time and place. An hour is a reasonable length of time – more can be intrusive, less is seldom long enough. Before ending the conversation go over your name, the date and time again, and don't forget to thank them.

✔ confirm the conversation in writing at once, taking care to say exactly what the purpose of the interview is

Even people who are very experienced interviewees can panic once the conversation is over, and decide, subsequently, that they've never met you or that you lied to them. I once asked a fellow journalist to tell me about his school days – not a very useful interview because, when I checked with the school, time had played tricks with his memory. A year later he wrote an article claiming, somewhat illogically, that I had used his life as the basis for the book's central character *and* got all the facts wrong.

✔ make short notes of the major areas you want to cover in the conversation. Don't write out entire questions. Your rapport with the interviewee is of paramount importance and long notes will be a distraction.

✔ always be polite, which includes being punctual but not early and not wasting their time.

✔ leave your ego outside – talk about yourself only in so far as it will help you build empathy with your subject.

✔ use a tape recorder, and make very brief notes at the same time to guide you in transcribing the tape. It is very rare for an interviewee to object to being taped, but frantically scribbling notes while they talk is off-putting.

✔ if your subject is inhibited, use the active-listening technique.

This means briefly rephrasing their replies, then waiting. All you do is encourage them to talk by letting them know that you really are listening. They say, 'I didn't like having a baby much.' You say, 'You didn't like having a baby.' You hope they will then amplify with something like, 'No, I didn't. I was in labour twenty-two hours, I was vomiting all the time, the anaesthetist was drunk, the pain was so bad it felt like someone dropped a red-hot iron bar on my stomach. I thought I was dying. They told me I bit the midwife, but all I remember was my husband asking me why I was making so much noise.'

✔ when you have covered your own agenda, ask if there's anything they would like to add

✔ write to express your thanks afterwards, acknowledge their help in the book and send them a copy of it

✔ label the tape and keep it for at least six months after the book is published

5) *Location*: There are very successful writers who research locations by buying a map and a few guide-books. Their novels do not give the reader a satisfying sense of place. Nothing is as good as visiting the places you intend to write about – it may be pleasurable, thrilling, deadly boring, frightening or the last thing your holiday companions want to do but it is always worthwhile. Even if you already know a place, try to revisit it specifically for your research.

It is important not to be a tourist. You want to get the feel of day-to-day life in the place, which means spending time hanging out, doing very little, soaking up information as well as actively observing. The big things about a place are easy to discover, the little things are what will make it real for your readers. Notice the climate changes at different times of day, listen to what people on the street say when they stop to talk, see how the children behave when they walk home from school.

Take photographs, because the camera will record information which your memory misses, and if you can, make drawings as well, because drawing a scene will make your eyes work harder. In certain places – courtrooms, theatres – photographs are forbidden and you'll have to draw, however bad you are at it. Record everyday sights – the buses, the shop-windows, the traffic cops. You never know what you'll need. Make notes to go with your visual references, but don't let note-taking interfere with your experience of the place. Label and date your records at the time you make them.

Copy James Bond and buy a local newspaper. Check out the bookshops, the libraries and local newspaper archives if you need them. Works which may be long out of print in your own country may still be in stock where they are of local significance. Some publishers even have small imprints dedicated to particular regions. Look for locally published material, recipes from the church magazine, booklets from the historical society.

My friends and family have been delighted to be dragged all over the world on research trips sold to them as holidays, but yours may not be so amenable. I financed some of my early research by writing travel articles but don't care to go as far as other authors of my acquaintance who begin by calling up the tourist office and demanding every available freebie, discount and privilege. On the whole, the less privileged you are as a traveller the more useful your experience will be.

6) Experiential Research: Like a method actor, you can use research to help the instinctive process of character creation, and put yourself through the same experiences as your protagonist. Until you have painted for two hours, you won't realise how much an artist's arm aches. Until you've run out of the players' tunnel at Wembley Stadium, you won't know how your heart beats when you first step out on to soccer's sacred turf.

It's particularly valuable to shadow someone who does your protagonist's job for a day (maybe more if they can bear it). Then you really appreciate where the stresses and strains of that occupation are. Just don't sit in the corner of someone's office noting every idiot thing they say on the telephone – that's being a writer for a day and you know how to do that. Help out if you are allowed to, act like a student on work experience and make yourself as useful as you can. Make notes every two or three hours, privately.

7) Double Checks: Checking your facts is the final phase of research and it is crucial. Apart from obvious things like words which are mumbled on an interview tape, there are also things which you need to verify.

A book can break the law in several ways – it can publish a libel, incite a criminal act or be liable for damages. Only an obviously sensitive book will be read by a publisher's lawyer, but your contract with your publisher will almost certainly contain a clause requiring you to ensure that your book is legal in every respect. You should not rely on your editor to do this, although she can help. Look through your synopsis with legality in mind and see if there is anything which you should modify, discard or investigate.

Take special care with anything which could lead – or mislead – a reader to do something harmful. Bear in mind that children and students are voracious readers of popular fiction and do not have a vast experience of life with which to interpret what they read. They do, however, have much more powerful emotions than the supposedly mature.

You can't put a Gladiator at the end of your book to say, 'Remember, kids, don't try these stunts at home!' You wouldn't if you could. What you can do is explore all the implications of what you intend your characters to do. When you have your information, consider how you can treat it responsibly. A mercenary soldier in Africa can be described going to sleep with his thumb on the pin of a live grenade because your reader can't zip out to Mr Patel's All-Nite Mart and pick up a six-pack of live grenades. But if you want to describe a death by some handy domestic means – like analgesic or weedkiller – it would be best to keep the detail some way short of a blueprint and work a public health commercial into the surrounding dialogue.

This research should be continued even after the book is published. In one of my novels a character injected a drug which was then known to straight medicine only as a rather unfashionable tranquilliser; my expert on recreational pharmacology mentioned that it had become a new cheap buzz popular with people who couldn't afford anything else. I consulted a doctor and a criminal psychologist, neither of whom had heard of this substance being used recreationally. By the time my book was published, a year later, this cheap buzz was *the* new thing on the street. By the time the paperback was about to go to print, injecting the cheap buzz was discovered to cause blocked blood vessels, strokes, gangrene leading to amputation and, on occasion, instant death, and the drug was withdrawn from the market. We had time to update the book before printing.

Putting It All Together

Here is an extract from *White Ice* in which research from seven different sources is used in a description of a woman voting in the Leningrad triple election held in 1990. Anya has been off-stage for 300 pages; we last saw her as a student in 1968, which was also the last time we visited Leningrad, so this is a substantial re-orientation exercise. The most important information in this passage is about Anya's attitudes, the mixture of bitterness and optimism which suggests that she has had a hard time since our last meeting.

Anya looked at the buff form in her hand. Three votes to be cast. Should the city be renamed St Petersburg – cross out the word no if you wanted the new name. Or rather, the old name. Would changing the name be an insult to Lenin? Who cared, what had Lenin ever done for her? Would keeping the name be an insult to St Peter? St Peter denied Christ; naturally, he was a man, don't men deny everything when it suits them?

She looked down at her red dress, creased in front and seated behind although she pressed it every day. It was made from poor-quality wool, reclaimed probably, there was no heart in it. In the real St Petersburg they had worn elegant clothes. This place was filthy, collapsing into its own mud, there was no food. A miracle it had survived so long. Maybe the new name would help. She crossed out 'No.'

Now, the party leader. Some self-righteous *babushka* on the metro had told the whole carriage that only gays, tarts and spivs would vote for Yeltsin. 'Sounds like everybody I know,' a young man had answered and the entire sardine-tin of people had laughed. They said that strangers met and fucked in the metro without anyone knowing, people were all jammed together so tightly. They said that every Russian woman was a prostitute. Anya preferred to call herself a free-trade zone. She voted for Yeltsin.

Lastly the mayor. Sobchak was a doll, he was a civilised

man, rational but not a fence-sitter. She loved watching him on television, that cute chipmunk smile, and the only one with brains. Last night he had said that the only thing worth working for was for your children and grandchildren to live in another society. She agreed with that. Anya had no living children and seven – no, eight – abortions. Not so bad, that was the average so there must be women with more. But it wasn't too late. And hadn't she been working on living in another society herself all her life?

She voted for Sobchak, folded her paper and posted it into the plain varnished wooden ballot box, giving the padlock a cynical pat. Of course the election was rigged but you had to go through the motions all the same.

It was the height of summer. Out by the sea the sweetish smell of the water was pleasant, but as they approached the city on the trolley-bus there was only the stink of dust and sweaty people. The air was like a steam bath and two cars with boiling radiators caused a traffic jam half a mile from the terminus. She struggled through the crush of passengers and jumped down to walk, pleased to have got away without putting her five kopecks in the ticket machine.

On the way to the hotel she saw a queue, not too long either, outside a meat shop. 'Not for those horrible Chernobyl chickens, is it?' she asked the last person. Any chicken was good to find these days, even the mutant ones with twisted beaks or a stump instead of a wing. He shrugged and grunted. People used to be kinder, now they never wanted to talk. She saw a woman leave with a round parcel. Even the radioactive birds were never that shape.

In forty minutes she saw with satisfaction that it was pork and bought all she could afford, snapping abuse at the women behind her. It wasn't rationed so why shouldn't she buy what she could?

Walking on to the free-enterprise market, she looked for cucumbers and potatoes; you could never count on anything these days. There were some cucumbers, but the price! Two years ago cucumbers were five roubles a kilo, but you paid anything for them now. The only ones left were malformed

> but she still had to fight over them with some pot-bellied young hooligan who thought he had the right to shoulder her aside just because he pissed standing up. No time to line up for potatoes, even if there were any. Sometimes she felt like hanging herself after queuing.

The buff form, the ballot box, the market prices, the belief that everyone in old St Petersburg was elegantly dressed and the opinion that only gays, tarts and spivs voted for Yeltsin all came from a TV documentary on the election. I spent ten days in Leningrad, and the decay of the city, the look of Anya's dress, the market goods, the smells, the meat queue, the traffic jam, the metro and the trolley-bus ride came mostly from my memory, rather than notes. Anya's view of Sobchak was extrapolated from a newspaper profile. Her cynicism, especially about men, and her number of abortions were inspired by my Russian friend's conversation and the statistic came from an official handbook. The observation about prostitution came from a book of interviews. The Chernobyl chicken and the sex on the metro were items in a TV report on a Leningrad satirist. All this information was filtered through Anya's state of mind, so that every fact tells you more about her, as well as about the city.

Notes and How to Make Them

An archive is only as good as its retrieval system. Notes for fiction are much harder to organise than notes for a factual book because there is no logical system of classification for them, nothing to determine when you will need to know what. You can spend a year on research and make thousands of pages of notes, but if you don't store them so that you can remember what you have and where to find it, your effort will be wasted.

For the very disciplined, chapter files work well. In a folder or a card index, you make a file for each chapter and, since you know approximately what area of the story you are going to cover in each, you can file your notes roughly at the start. Get *all* the notes out and re-read them as you begin each chapter, otherwise you can finish with something crucial still forgotten at the back of the file. As writing progresses, anything unused is moved forward to the chapter containing the next situation to which it could be relevant. As the chapter structure is modified, the notes will be reallocated again. It can be laborious, but it works if you have the patience.

Writers who are computer-literate and have the technology for split screens can work the same system on disc. Notes made on computer files need to be copied and printed out as insurance against the day there is a power cut or a virus or some other inevitable but unimaginable disaster. Writers who merely dabble with word-processing are best advised to work from notes on paper, because the operation of clearing the screen to retrieve research is much more time-consuming.

A very simple system of accessing research avoids taking notes from books at all. As you read, put paper slips in your books to mark important information, with a note of the page number and subject on each. Compile a detailed subject index, either on paper or on disc. When you are writing, keep the books on or near your desk, and with the help of the index go back to the relevant text when you need it. A great advantage of this method is that it gives you the facts in context. It is a very good system for people whose thinking is scattered rather than linear, but since those minds are also the most highly distractible it does offer a dangerous amount of temptation.

Strange But True

Ahmed wrapped the silver in canvas, buried it under the bungalow, and followed the terse order of the British governors to the native population – *pergu ulu*, go into the jungle. Ah Kit, Gerald's boy, took the wheels off the Model T and put wood blocks under the axles. He left with Ahmed, the picture of dejection.

'Cheer up, man,' Ahmed told him as they turned their backs on the plantation. 'There'll always be an England.'

PEARLS

I discovered that jaunty reassurance, overheard in real life in a conversation between two Malay houseboys on the eve of the fall of Singapore, in an oral history of the colonial Far East. That did not make it sound any more credible to my novel's editor, who wanted to delete it and only gave way because it was a minor exchange.

Fact is stranger than fiction. In the course of your research you will turn up facts that don't fit, and be particularly delighted with them on that account: 'Wow! Imagine that! A person being stabbed doesn't feel anything sharp at all, they feel as if they've been thumped with something blunt. Wow!'

People have their own ideas of how things are supposed to be. In the case of the bar rail discussed earlier, any reader of reasonable visual awareness would have expected a chrome rail in a cocktail bar; brass rails are more typical in pubs. When you come to use information which conflicts with widespread perceptions, it needs to be carefully introduced, giving the reader time to adjust to the new picture. However correct you may be, if you simply give a fact that contradicts your readers' expectation, they will assume that you are wrong and you will lose their confidence.

Sometimes the fact doesn't fit because things look different on television. To a scuba-diver, a coral reef is mostly dim shades of blue-grey, because so much natural light is reflected by the surface of the water that only the slow end of the spectrum can be seen below. To a couch potato, a coral reef is a brilliant mass of neon-yellow butterfly fish, green-lipped clams, red-and-white Spanish dancer worms, ultramarine starfish, pink-tailed wrasse, orange fire-coral, lavender fans and leopard-spotted dragon eels. If you want to take a couch potato down 30 metres off the Great Barrier Reef without blowing your credibility, you will need to break the news that all those colours only show up under the lights used for underwater filming.

And Finally . . .

Keep your notes, notebooks, tapes, sketches, videos, maps and everything else except the library books for at least six months after your book is published. After six months, a legal action for libel can no longer be brought but if – perish the thought – you were to be sued for anything else your notes would be essential evidence. The fact that you know that you wrote your own book would have no weight at all if you were sued for plagiarism.

There are many envious, deluded and exploitative characters out there. Millions of people around the world share the same experiences, receive the same information and watch the same news footage on TV every night. The same ideas occur to millions of people at about the same time – if it were not so, stories addressing those ideas would have small significance. Of those millions, a few hundred will have followed the same thought process as you, and probably got as far as putting their ideas down on paper. If one of those few hundred felt badly because you were published and apparently making money, and he was not, and he had perhaps already submitted his idea to an agent or publisher who had some connection with you, he could be advised to take legal action against you. To defend yourself, you would need to demonstrate not only that your ideas were your own, but when and how you formed them.

5

The Hero's Journey – Planning

A good story is obviously a difficult thing to invent, but
its difficulty is a poor reason for despising it

THE SUMMING UP
W Somerset Maugham

One Story, One Plan

You know the whole story already. So do your readers. The
shape of a story is imprinted on our collective unconscious.
Perhaps it is inborn, barcoded somewhere in our DNA; perhaps
we learn it, from the stories we hear over and over again from
our cradles.

Reading a book is picking out a path which we have taken
before but can't quite remember. We do not wander aimlessly
in a story, but explore it purposefully, alert for signs, ready for
surprises, not sure of our destination but confident that we will
know it when we get there.

Writing the story is the same process: setting off with a
beginning, an end of some kind in view, a few scenes expected,
but most of the journey a succession of unknown possibilities.

Some writers begin only with a character and find their way *by* the character, creating situations to test it. With time and thought, the path becomes clearer and clearer until it is a fully realised narrative.

The journey is easier with a map. The map is what we have in our unconscious, the central story of every heroic myth, a form found all over the world, in every culture and at every time. A story can be like a virgin forest – once you get inside it you get disoriented. What looked like a path disappears, every vista is the same and once you turn around you no longer know which way you were facing before. With a map, you can still get lost in your story, but it is easier to get back on track. Using the map strengthens the planning process, allowing your story to fill out to its maximum power, testing the characters and extending your ideas to their logical limits.

Why Plan?

Writing is an art in which technique is despised in some quarters. As painters are no longer taught to draw and dance 'graduates' advised that there is no need to bother with line or turn-out, authors are encouraged to follow Lytton Strachey, who believed that writing should be like running through a field. Even when running through a field, you need to look where you are going (and Lytton Strachey did not write fiction). In bestsellers, writers are the direct heirs of the novelists of the nineteenth century, concerned with the material of human life and the classical structure which that dictates – a beginning, a middle and an end.

Something happened between *Pride and Prejudice* and *The Name of the Rose*. The contribution of the twentieth century has been to develop an audience so sophisticated, so hotly aware of dramatic structure, that the simple linear narrative can be doubled, tripled, knotted and cat's-cradled as writer and readers enjoy elaborate games of anticipation and surprise. We are an audience trained by visual media, by television, film and commercials, an audience which is perfectly comfortable with

35 concurrent plot lines and near-subliminal images. In fact, we love all that. The sound-bite definition of the technique by film director Jean-Luc Godard was, 'A beginning, a middle and an end – but not necessarily in that order.' All this is easier if you plan it.

What is an Outline?

All artists plan their work. Painters make sketches, sculptors make models, composers write drafts, actors rehearse. Authors write outlines. An outline is a simple plan of a book, a sketch, a model, a story-board; its purpose is to find out if your ideas work, to discover whether your story is a sound, functional creation. In outlining your book you discover the flaws in the story and correct them.

Any artist would prefer to identify weaknesses in his conception at the outset because it is much more difficult to put things right when the work is in progress. Writers, however, are a law unto themselves. Many writers do not consider planning a normal preliminary exercise; they think it is an interference with the creative process. People who, as students, always planned their essays, feel that as professional writers they should plan no more. Perhaps because writing is the most conscious, least instinctive of creative fields, the almost superstitious dread of construction is cherished by way of compensation.

Planning a book does not mean imposing a structure on your ideas. It means discovering what the structure of your ideas really is. Planning means refining your narrative to an outline of its events and, in that process, freeing your instinct from the contortions which your intellect has forced upon it. In the depths of your mind your story is already perfectly formed. When you come to tell it, the story has to pass through your personal wishes and fears, the accumulated patterns of other writers' work and the mass of received ideas about what should and should not happen in a book, before it emerges and takes on its own life in the mind of your reader. Your task is to be the story's midwife, to bring it out whole and undeformed.

The Two Perils

Scylla and Charybdis were the two perils threatening ships in the narrow straits between Italy and the island of Sicily. They were on opposite sides of the passage – if you steered away from one, you steered towards the other. According to Homer, Scylla was a huge rock guarded by a six-headed sea monster and Charybdis a vast whirlpool which sucked up the whole sea and spewed it out again three times a day. The experienced pilot steered straight down the middle and avoided them both.

Planning a story means charting the same nicely judged kind of course. Your Scylla is the disdain for construction which infects the higher realms of literature. Anthony Burgess, reviewing my first novel, praised the degree to which it engaged his interest despite the fact that he was watching the Monte Carlo Grand Prix on TV at the same time, then remarked that 'plot, as T S Eliot said, is only the bone that you throw at the dog that feeds on narrative while the real work of literature proceeds.'

The belief that plot is a distraction (and that anyone who follows it is a dog) is ridiculous but common. The arch-believers are so rabid that they claim to be able to detect a book written on a word-processor because it 'tastes of construction'. Absurd and primitive as this superstition may be, I have seen it published in quality newspapers which would treat reports of vampires in the streets with derision but are respectfully receptive to the ravings of distinguished literary figures.

The plot of a book is simply the author's ideas expressed as events. The plot is the form which gives the story its universal significance, as well as the pointer which directs the reader's interest. This is the real work of literature. Everything else is decoration; without a plot a book has no meaning, it is a work of intellectual titillation which is culturally inert.

Disdain for narrative accompanies literary aspiration and is thus widespread among publishers, writers and reviewers. This body of opinion holds that popular fiction must be 'plot-driven' or 'narrative-led', but produces editors with no great under-standing of narrative structure. Such an editor will lightly propose removing the foundation scene of a plot, without which the whole house falls down, or advancing the story twenty years so that the essential social conditions for the story no longer exist. Your outline will help you stand your ground.

Writers on Scylla's side never plan. They just sit down with the germ of an idea and write a book from beginning to end. A few of them have minds like jewelled Swiss clockwork and produce stories of perfect craftsmanship. Those of less intricate intellectual endowment are the infanticides of literature and they suffer horribly. 'When you're a writer you have to kill your babies,' they boast, describing how another 50,000 words were junked because they became irrelevant. They succumb to power-mad characters who take over their plots, or sub-plots which proliferate like rogue viruses. They get very depressed, often lose heart and have drawers stuffed with half-completed books. Their novels are waffly, broken-backed accounts of nothing in particular which drive readers crazy. They do not write bestsellers.

Steering away from Scylla too violently will plunge you into Charybdis, the whirlpool of total structure, where you will be sucked into a hideous vortex of high concepts and laws of conflict and spewed out in a mess of beats, scenes, acts, story points, crises, climaxes and *dei ex machina*.

Navigators on the Charybdis side like to argue about how many plots there are, like the medieval ecclesiastics who argued about the number of angels who could dance on the head of a pin. They are considerably more ambitious than Aristotle, who suggested only two basic plots, or Goethe, with his modest estimate of five. Author and media lecturer Robert B Tobias defines twenty 'master' plots: Quest, Adventure, Pursuit, Rescue, Escape, Revenge, The Riddle, Rivalry, Underdog, Temptation, Metamorphosis, Transformation, Maturation, Love, Forbidden Love, Sacrifice, Discovery, Wretched Excess, Ascension and Descension. Rudyard Kipling holds the record for the largest number of plots ever defined – sixty-nine. Any such system of classification would probably be valid, but of no use to a writer. They are only ways of labelling stories, not techniques of creation.

Survivors of Charybdis feel they have to write according to rules, such as: a book should be around 180,000 words long; the composition of a book should be one-third action, one-third dialogue and one-third description; 25% of the action should take place over the first third of the book; the first-act crisis should be reversed in the second act. The fact is that most bestselling authors have never heard of these rules, and most bestselling books, especially the great ground-breaking popular novels, do not conform to them. In technical terms, some of the most influential books are seriously flawed but have exceptional strengths which mask their weaknesses. Structure alone does not make a bestseller.

Furthermore, nobody ever stopped at a bookstall and asked, 'Have you got something in World War II stories, around 80 or 100 events, with a reformation plot, an up ending and a sympathetic protagonist with blue eyes, cowboy boots and a pet iguana?'

The total-structure approach has largely been developed by academics, not by writers. It works from external to internal. Many modern novels could be improved by more careful construction, but it is a technique, and as such a discipline through which the creative process operates, not the process itself. The total-structure approach is so conscious that it blocks the imagination. Emotionally, it is sterile. It is a philosophy which does not honour the mystery of creation. It also regards readers as dogs, dumb creatures who can be trained.

Total structure is an effective method of producing hacks, and a useful training for instinctive storytellers whose natural gift is already too well developed to be suppressed, but writers who believe that structure is all produce books which are incapable of touching the emotions of their readers.

American editors are great worshippers of structure; the good ones are great, the majority have that weary, reductive approach to stories which would rate *Othello* as a fairly interesting revenge scenario − if Bill could lose the racism and the history and work up something around the O J Simpson story.

Even with the most meticulous planning, an author can lose their way in a book from a very early stage and end up with a story that occasionally stumbles. An editor with a flair for structure can be a saviour, but there are very few of them in European publishing: in television and film, script editors, directors and producers regard construction as of paramount importance but in books the nearest equivalent is the editor with a smattering of structural principles who will relentlessly attempt to sanitise, sweeten or sensationalise your story on the grounds that this is the right thing to do with 'books like this'. Every now and then one of these misguided fools writes a novel. The novel is technically perfect and commercially disastrous. They wonder why.

Mozart or Beethoven?

Most people want to be like Mozart, who just wrote down the music he heard in his head and produced beautiful clean manuscripts with very little sign of revision. Nobody wants to be Beethoven, whose scores are dark with deletions, whole passages crossed out with thick lines, rewritten over and over again, as if every note had to be dragged in agony from the depths of his tormented mind.

A well-known agent recently recommended the Beethoven method as the only way for a writer to draft a story, insisting that a huge, laborious schedule of multiple revisions was essential. It is not. All that is essential is to construct a good plot. How you do that is immaterial; whether you figure it out mentally or work it out on paper is of no consequence. I suspect that Mozart revised just as much as Beethoven, but did so in his head, while Beethoven put the whole process on paper.

The Ten Stages

The core structure of every story is the heroic journey of mythology. It is a quest for enlightenment, the legend of life and how to live it. It's a fairy tale symbolising the search for unity with the self. The hero can be a woman or a man, it makes no difference, the journey is always the same, and has the same elements – all over the world, in every culture, in every age. I have grouped them under ten headings.

Understanding the elements of the heroic journey is a powerful aid to developing a plot. As your story takes shape and you identify the elements which have spontaneously appeared in it, you will understand the progress of your hero and, if your invention falters, you will have a basic model for what the next step on the journey should be.

The technique works whether you begin with a full narrative, a single episode, a theme or just one character. Not every story contains every element, and the elements appear in different order, with different emphasis, in each story. In ancient mythology the whole length of the journey was only covered in long story cycles; the individual tales in the cycle each covered a short section. In modern mythology there is no need to tell the whole story because if the fragment you give the audience is powerful enough they will fill in the rest for themselves.

The elements of the heroic journey are your primary colours; the whole picture of life proceeds from them.

1) The Opening

At the start of the story, the hero is in a static situation, within a family or society or state of mind which is stable, but which no longer nourishes him spiritually. It is an inauthentic state in which his true self cannot function. He is inert and inactive. This is the life which will be left behind, the childhood world of parental authority and borrowed values, the old self which must be discarded.

At the start the hero is often at some sort of personal nadir, like James Bond before his adventures begin, demotivated and unfit, or sunk in cynical apathy like Philip Marlowe. He may simply lack the courage to move forward. Sometimes, as in *The Empire of the Sun*, he is literally a child, in the care and control of his parents.

Some heroes are physically restrained – tied up, locked in or weighed down – by something which is a symbol of the restriction of their spirit. At the start of Judith Krantz's *Scruples*, the heroine, Billie Ikehorn, is insulated in fat, a wretchedly lonely, freakishly obese teenager, the despair of her family and pariah of her school.

2) The Call to Adventure

This is the point when the journey begins. An event, perhaps a meeting or a discovery, destabilises the world of the hero and obliges him to set out in search of a new equilibrium.

Sometimes the hero's world is destroyed outright and he has no choice but to leave. The parents die, the wife walks out, the husband deserts, the business goes bust, she gets fired, he is given six months to live – something happens to challenge the hero and he has to respond. In *The Hitchhiker's Guide to the Galaxy*, the Earth itself is destroyed, blown up to make way for a hyperspace expressway, obliging Arthur Dent to set out into space.

Sometimes, the challenge is a person, a meeting. In *The Bridges of Madison County*, a stranger, Robert Kincaid, draws up at Francesca's farm in Iowa and asks her the way to the covered bridge:

> 'You're pretty close. The bridge is only about two miles from here.' Then, after twenty years of living the close life, a life of circumscribed behaviour and hidden feelings demanded by a rural culture, Francesca Johnson surprised herself by saying, 'I'll be glad to show it to you, if you want.'
> Why she did that she had never been sure.

The call is always irresistible. The meeting is with the person who will be the hero's guide on the adventure of life, a figure who appears instantly fascinating, a meeting with a strong sense of destiny around it.

3) Response or Refusal

Francesca Johnson answers her challenge at once, but other heroes need more than one invitation to break out of their old selves. In John Grisham's *The Firm*, the call comes when an FBI man approaches Mitch, a young lawyer, at lunch in a Greek deli, but he chooses to ignore the first warning. Mitch is greedy – the opposing quality in his character which first led him to take his job with a law firm even more conventional than he himself is. His conventional concern for his livelihood takes him through successive approaches from the FBI, until his superiors try to enforce his loyalty by blackmail and he finally takes action.

When the hero answers the call to adventure, his quest has begun. At this point he sets aside his old ambitions and forms a new goal, the pursuit of which will lead him through the succeeding events to a new level of self-knowledge.

4) The Guide

This is the first positive encounter on the hero's journey, the meeting with a protective figure who gives the traveller advice, charms or weapons to help him. The figure of the guide represents the benign and protective forces of destiny, the reassurance that the hero has only to trust and success will follow. In myths the guide is often an old woman or an old man. In *Star Wars* it was Obi-Wan Kenobi, who taught Luke Skywalker about the Jedi knights and the Force. In two of John Le Carré's spy stories the guide is Connie Sachs, the retired head of secret service research, whom George Smiley consults almost like an oracle for the key to the mysteries he must solve.

The guide is a conduit for the life force who acts like a priest or a shaman but does not necessarily appear in that form, although Robert Kincaid is actually described as 'a magician of sorts' and 'looking like some vision from a never-written book called *An Illustrated History of Shamans*'. Often the guide is a lover, an instinctive personality who unlocks the human core of the hero and reconnects him with life.

5) The Threshold Guardian

This is the first negative encounter, the first antagonist, who meets the hero as he is about to leave his known world and enter the unexplored, supernatural realm outside. The threshold guardian points out the dangers ahead, stresses the comfort of the known world, tries to persuade the hero to remain.

Sometimes the guardian is well-meaning and intends to be protective, but nonetheless is still operating from the old world which must be left behind. In mythology the guardian is often deceptive or seductive, a false friend sent to mislead the hero into danger. In *Fatherland* the guardian is the hero's close colleague, Max Jaeger, an older, fatter, tireder man, a Party member, no less intelligent than the hero and no less conscience-stricken, but afraid. Jaeger is focused on a last promotion and a peaceful retirement, on his beer and cigars and the chance of getting home early to his wife Hannelore, Holder of the Honour Cross of the German Mother, Bronze Class (happily, we never meet her). Jaeger is at the hero's side throughout the story, urging him to give up:

> Take some leave man. I'm serious. You need a rest ... come home and have supper with me and Hannelore. You look as if you haven't had a decent meal in weeks. The Gestapo have taken the file. The autopsy report is going straight to Prinz-Albrecht Strasse. It's over. Done. Forget it.

6) The Void

The heroic myth is a story of death and rebirth, death of the old self, rebirth as a new being. The hero enters the void at the point where he has discarded his old self – his old values or ways of behaving – but not yet grown his new identity. This is a fallow period, a time of withdrawal, even exile, a dark winter of the soul in which the seeds of the new life begin to germinate.

In *The Thorn Birds*, by Colleen McCulloch, the void is the heroine's marriage, a period of increasing suffering at the hands of a cruel and avaricious man during which the confused emotions of her adolescence resolve into the certainty of her love for the ambitious priest.

In the *Angelique* series, which was created by a husband and wife writing together as Sergeanne Golon, the heroine enters the void immediately after her second trial, when her husband is executed as a heretic and she herself hunted by the Inquisition. In a sequence which occupies almost half the second book, she literally falls among thieves, into the degraded Paris underworld centred on the Tour de Nesle, inhabited by criminals, beggars and madmen. Here her old identity is obliterated and she is forced into the depths of her own character, gathering the strength to set out again and combat her enemies.

In *Gone With The Wind* the void period is equally harsh, the time after Scarlett's return to Tara to face starvation and the destruction of her home and family. At the end of this exile, however, Scarlett's old identity reasserts itself.

7) The Trials and The Helpers

This section of the journey corresponds to what a script editor would describe as the second act of the drama, a succession of conflicts building towards the crisis and climax. Once the hero sets out again, he has to survive a series of ordeals, or defeat a succession of antagonists. This phase is a series of initiation rites for the new self, a testing period which symbolises a journey through the internal darkness of the psyche.

The ground covered represents a spiritual landscape, in which the figures are frequently instructive, giving the hero clues as to what he must do to be victorious. As well as antagonists, there are benign helpers in this passage who give the hero their knowledge, wisdom or gifts.

In this part of the journey the hero travels faster and faster, gaining power (strength, support or knowledge) after each trial, becoming more and more certain of his goal. The action widens across the canvas of the story, involving more people, wider circles of society. It also deepens into the character of the protagonist – in taking your hero across this ground, keep asking, 'What is the worst thing that can happen to him now?' The purpose is to extract from the character the last crumb of resolve, the last ounce of conviction that his cause is just, the last drop of morale for the last battle.

In *Fatherland* the hero encounters a series of antagonists who are fearsome but predictable – his corrupt colleagues in the criminal police, SS officers, a Gestapo general, the head of the criminal police. His final antagonist, however, is his own ten-year-old son, whose betrayal makes the overthrow of the Nazi regime a personal imperative strong enough for him to resist the interrogation which follows.

8) The Crisis – The Mystical Marriage

This is a single point in the story at which the hero, pushed to his limit, makes the decision which will create the climax and so frame the end of the story. It is a moment of revelation, when the central character finally understands the game and with this new consciousness makes the right decision. In psychological terms, the choice is made at the moment when he is fully and completely his new self, able to act in complete unity with his reborn spirit.

In ancient myths the moment is often represented as a marriage between a human and an immortal, a union which symbolises the human's mastery of life and victory over death. In novels the metaphor can be a transforming relationship, in which the hero unites with a lover of opposing cardinal quality and becomes complete. (Remember this is art, not life. In life, of course, the hero unites with a lover of opposing cardinal quality and bitches about it forever.)

9) The Climax – The Supreme Ordeal

This is the final conflict on the hero's journey, which takes place as a consequence of the crisis decision. In action stories both the crisis and climax are usually clearly distinguished and strongly foreshadowed at the opening of the book. The climax is an event which has a strong sense of destiny about it, because the reader has expected it from the start.

The conflict symbolises an atonement with the father, the authority figure who has been supplanted by the hero. At the opening of the story this authority held sway in the hero's life, and so its overthrow has been expected from the moment the journey began. However, it must be clear that the new authority of the hero is equal to ordering the world of the story, that his power is sufficiently great for him to rule.

In emotional stories, where the greatest conflicts are internal, the crisis and climax may not be so apparent, but they follow the same pattern. Throughout *The Thorn Birds* the central character, Meggie, has loved possessively and painfully. She reacts to the death of her son by revealing to her one-time lover, now a cardinal, that the child was his, and in consequence brings about his death too. It is the final figure of the pattern of her life, in which whatever she has sought to possess she has driven away. From this last trial she gains the wisdom to set her remaining child, a daughter, free of her love, thereby breaking the cycle and gaining peace.

Some central characters lose the last battle, which turns the story into a tragedy – although in spiritual terms the journey has still been completed. Scarlett O'Hara twice refuses her calls to adventure, but when the Civil War destroys her world her next actions – saving Tara and her family, rebuilding her life – lead us to believe that she will change. In fact she does not; Scarlett never willingly responds to the call. A terrible dissembler, she even fakes for the reader, and only appears to change. In fact, she remains selfish to the last and when Rhett demands the gift of herself, she refuses, in fact becoming worse than she ever was. The death of her child and the death of Rhett's love follow; her enlightenment is achieved, but too late.

10) The Return
This is the final phase of the journey, one which is often only hinted at in modern stories, in which the hero, now reborn, brings back the wisdom he has learned to transform his old world and do good to his old associates. He may be pursued, and he may have to struggle to recross the threshold, but on his arrival he will appear as a god among men.

This is the long stroll into the sunset, the extended happy-ever-after which was mandatory in nineteenth-century novels but which is now considered trite and diminishing to the main story. It is usually confined to a passage of resolution, in which any remaining sub-plots can be resolved and the last lingering questions of 'what happened to . . .?' are answered. In films this is sometimes done behind the closing titles.

This is also a time to bring on the characters who pass judgement on the action or emphasise its meaning. The effects of the climax in the outer world can be indicated and the readers allowed to recover their emotional balance.

At the end of *The Firm*, Mitch has co-operated with the FBI and negotiated his safe escape to the Caribbean with his wife and brother. There, sitting under a palm tree on the beach sipping rum punch, they read the newspaper reports detailing the indictment of his former employers, along with a large number of Chicago mafiosi whose money the firm existed to launder. They remain terrified of mob retribution, but manage to agree that they could have done worse than end up cruising the Caribbean with eight million dollars in the bank.

The Forbidden God

There is only one thing which is absolutely forbidden in constructing a plot, and that is the device called *deus ex machina*. *Deus ex machina* is a thundering great coincidence which just happens to solve all the hero's problems instantly. In life, this happens. People do win the lottery, villains do die in plane crashes, whole families are wiped out in avalanches, childhood sweethearts do meet again on the street 25 years after the ghastly misunderstanding which parted them, and it turns out that they are both single, both solvent, both sane, both still in love with each other and they live happily ever after.

Life is not a story. In a story, *deus ex machina* is forbidden because the audience never believes it. The audience never believes it because they are following the hero's journey, in which no progress is ever made except as a consequence of the hero's actions. Accidents may happen to the hero, but how he responds determines what happens next. *Deus ex machina* events make the hero superfluous. Given the psychological dynamics of a story, *deus ex machina* events suggest that enlightenment is irrelevant, self-knowledge pointless. This may be so, but it is not what the readers wish to believe, or they would never open books at all.

The term *deus ex machina* is a little misleading. It is supposed to derive from a device of the ancient Greek theatre, in which Olympus was a high platform from which the gods were lowered by machinery to intervene in human lives. This suggests that in Greek drama plots were resolved by chance, which is not so. The original *dei ex machina* were archetypal figures symbolising human qualities, and their appearance externalised the internal dramas of the characters.

Outline Methods

Drafting by hand on paper will, of course, produce a Beethoven-like mess of scribbles, brackets and arrows. Much of the revision process involves moving scenes around, changing their order until the profile or rhythm of the story seems right; some people draft on an A4 student pad, then cut the pages into scenes, switch them around and tape them together in their final running order, which is then rewritten with Mozartian clarity. Until they change their minds.

A neater, more flexible way is the card method: writing a brief outline of each scene on an index card or postcard, then laying them out – on the floor if necessary – and shuffling the pack until the order is right. If a scene extends itself too much for the rhythm of your story, divide it onto two cards. Number the cards in a top corner in pencil and keep them together with the high-tech device of a rubber band. Sub-plots can be put on different coloured cards. You can change your mind as much as you like, all you need to do is take off the band and shuffle again.

Dale Spender described the word-processor as 'glamour cut-and-paste'. Drafting on a WP is extremely easy, although with a very complex plot you may find that the limitation of the screen size is a handicap. Sub-plots can be shown with different fonts. You can change your mind to infinity.

I did once hear a professor of poetry, who ought to have known better, insist that word-processors are a bad thing because you cannot keep your drafts; this is, of course, just another of those Luddite superstitions cherished only by grand academics. If you really want to keep every single version of your narrative, you can save them all on disk. A sensible person would save the master draft and copy it. The paranoid would save it, copy it and print it out as well. Those whose paranoia comes with hallucinations of fire gutting the writing room can keep the copy disk in another room. I do actually know a writer who lost his work when his house was flooded.

Beyond The Outline

At the end of the outline process you should have a summary of the linear narrative of your book. You can begin writing with confidence at this point and make any further structural alterations during the writing, or after the story is completed, using your outline to model them. Unless your novel has been commissioned on the basis of an outline, you are not obliged to stick to it and can revise it as you go along. However, it is wise to keep the original plan so that you can refer back to it to remind yourself why you decided to take that particular course in the first place – the brilliant ideas which come along while you are writing may, in fact, destabilise the plot.

Writers who work in a very structured way sometimes plan further before they begin. You can use the outline to decide in what order the beginning, the middle and the end of the story should be told; often the chronological progression does not seem quite intriguing enough. Effective complications are a prologue which enters the story just before the crisis point, or a prologue which takes place after the return. A prologue can also give the reader some of the central character's back story and an indication of how they got to their opening state.

With an overview of the plot, you can now consider the level of arousal to which your story will take your readers. To you the plot is an intellectual exercise; to your readers it will be an emotional roller-coaster ride. You may recall a roller-coaster ride from your last experience: the long, long, *long* beginning going up, up, up, up, *up*, until the passengers' sense of anticipation is almost unbearable; the first short plunge to get everyone screaming; the crescendo of ghastly manoeuvres during which you wonder why you ever agreed to go on the damned thing, swear you will never do it again and feel in serious danger of throwing up your lunch; the ominous level cruise when you are almost persuaded that the ordeal is over, and the final hideous cardiac-arresting plunge before the end.

While the thrill of anticipation is the same in a book, you have more than gravity to play with in creating your highs and lows. Surprise, sex and horror are all highly exciting elements – but not if they appear constantly, or always in the same form, or if they fail to turn up when expected. Humour, information and description are calming episodes, like the small drops and the flat runs, restorative and diversionary. Again, they need to be distributed in the right places.

Chapter divisions can be decided now. The right place to end a chapter is something you can feel, but the principle of chapter-ending, as with scene-changing in drama, is to cut the narrative at a point where the audience is desperate to know more, thereby increasing their suspense. The place to cut is just before the climax of a scene, when the hero has been challenged or crossed, when a conflict is inevitable, when a new piece of information has reframed the whole story. The reader immediately anticipates what will happen, whereupon the writer switches to something else and leaves that anticipation to build.

Sub-Plots and Story-Lines

At the outline stage you can add counterpoint to the main story with subsidiary story-lines or sub-plots. These should never be pure decoration. They must either reinforce the theme by displaying its operation in another form, or add diversion, but finally they will feed into the core story.

In books whose perspective on the world is wide, in which

several major characters are followed in several story-lines, each character is treated as a protagonist, with their own heroic journey to complete. The characters have to meet at the right time and in the right place – that is, with a credible reason for being there.

Action stories, in which humour would detract from the weight of the main narrative, and love stories, where the ridiculous needs to be segregated for the sake of credibility, often banish the laughs to a sub-plot. In drama it is considered desirable for all the sub-plots to be resolved before the climax, so that nothing can detract from the impact of the final scene. In a book, however, sub-plots can be resolved afterwards, although tying up more than one set of loose ends at that time can be awkward.

Visual Planning

If you are handy with graphs, you can depict the successive climaxes of the main story by plotting emotional impact against time, then adding lines for subsidiary story-lines and sub-plots in different colours. Go for a wall-chart if you want to get really fancy.

There is another method of visual analysis which can help to harness all the events of the plot to the theme – the mind-map. At times the characters in a story can stand around unhelpfully like strangers at a cocktail party, refusing to interact at any but the most superficial level. They seem to have no reason to be there. Analysing the story with a mind-map can help you get a grip on your ideas, so your characters start to move purposefully again. It is a particularly valuable exercise for writers who love characterisation but hate plotting, whose brains fog the minute they ask themselves what they are trying to say, who are much more taken with the infinite curiousness of human nature than with what implications those curiosities might have in action.

Draw a mind-map in pencil on an empty page. At the centre, write the theme of your book and draw an oval around it.

From that oval, draw a line for each major character, name it, and note how that character's values relate to the theme.

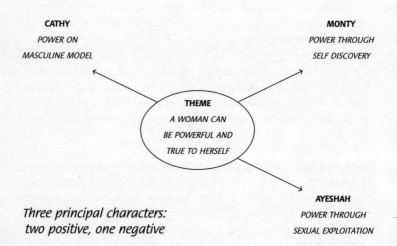

*Three principal characters:
two positive, one negative*

Then begin to mark the major events in the character's life, in each of which they will express their values, and thus their relationship to the theme. These branch off the first line. If you cannot fit an event on to the mind-map, it is not material to your story. You can mention it in passing, but keep it out of the core narrative.

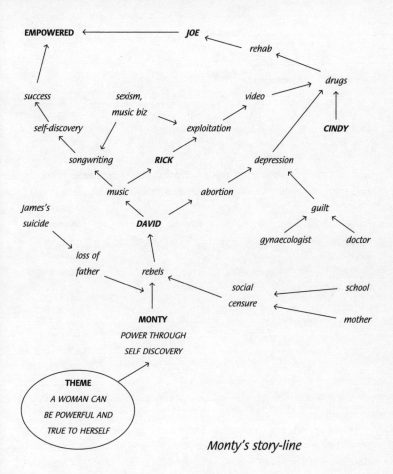

Monty's story-line

Finally, add in the small details of the character's actions. You should be able to find a place for everything – how they cut their hair, how much weight they carry, their favourite TV show. The map will now show everything the character does feeding back to the theme of the story. If there is an event that you cannot fit on to the mind-map, lose it – it is excess baggage.

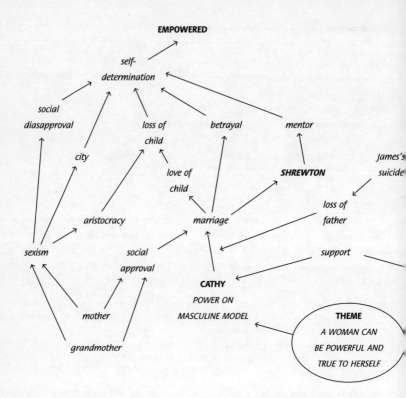

PEARLS – the mind-map in full

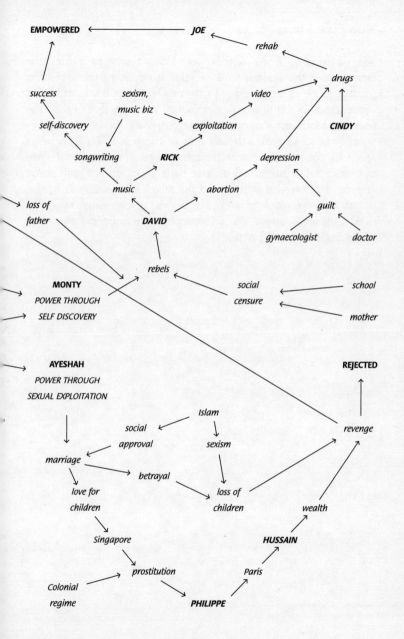

The Five Plans

The document from which you now begin to write, the summary of the main events of your story, is a *working outline*. In the course of its progress to the reader, your book will need other kinds of outline – sometimes as many as five. From the working outline, you can prepare a *writing schedule*, a motivational aid to structure the writing of the book. To interest an agent in your work you will need a *short selling outline*. If you intend to sell your novel on the basis of an outline and some sample chapters you will need a *full selling outline*. If you intend to submit your book to a film or television company, you may need a *dramatic outline*. These documents are discussed in greater detail in Chapter 12 (*see* p221).

6

Turning Pages

'Make 'em laugh. Make 'em cry. But most of all –
make 'em *wait*.'

William Goldman

Compulsive. Compelling. Gripping. Irresistible. Enthralling.
Unputdownable. Page-turning. Keeps you guessing to the end.
You'll stay up reading it all night.

That's the theory – what about the practice? How does a
story acquire such power that the reader will not be able to
sleep until it's finished? Assuming that the three big choices
have been made well – the story takes place in a significant
location, with characters with whom readers can become deeply
involved, and expresses a deep life-affecting wish – what
remains are the techniques for intensifying the reader's concentration. These are in the writer's toolbox, the craft skills which
can be taught, learned and practised.

ANCHORS

Readers need to feel oriented in a story. If they lose the sense
of where they are, who they are reading about, what people
look like, what time of day it is or what the climate is like
they feel uncomfortable, confused and bored – without really

knowing why. They will give up reading if they lose their sense of physical orientation.

Introduction

First impressions count. When you introduce a character or a place, tell the readers the most significant things they need to know about them quickly:

> He was six feet tall with virile good looks. Thick black hair worn just a tad too long, penetrating green eyes, a two-day stubble on a deep suntan and a hard body. He was thirty-nine years old and he had the world by the balls.
>
> Jack Python was one of the most famous talk-show hosts in America.
>
> HOLLYWOOD HUSBANDS
> *Jackie Collins*

This first meeting is important, and the description can run to a greater length here than anywhere later in the book. The full portrait of the Drogheda Estate in *The Thorn Birds* is more than two pages long. This is just an extract:

> Even to an Irishman used to castles and mansions, the Australian homestead was imposing. Drogheda was the oldest and biggest property in the district, and it had been endowed by its late doting owner with a fitting residence. Built of butter-yellow sandstone blocks hand-hewn in quarries five hundred miles eastward, the house had two storeys and was constructed on austerely Georgian lines, with large, many-paned windows and a wide, iron-pillared veranda running all the way round its bottom storey . . . Several acres of meticulously scythed lawn surrounded the house, strewn with formal gardens even now full of colour from roses, wallflowers, dahlias and marigolds. A stand of magnificent ghost gums with pallid white trunks and drifting leaves hanging seventy feet above the ground shaded the house

from the pitiless sun . . . Thanks to the late Michael Carson's passion for Drogheda homestead, he had been lavish in the matter of water tanks; rumor had it Drogheda could afford to keep its lawns green and its flower beds blooming though no rain fell in ten years.

Pictures Worth a Thousand Words

Light travels faster than sound. In most people's minds, visual information overrides the information from all the other senses. Readers want to picture the action of a story and need visual information to do so.

Colours, shapes and dimensions are vital, elaboration is not. Your purpose is to tempt your reader's imagination, not kill it with excess detail. Writers can be inclined to be control freaks, determined that every reader shall see the scene in exactly the same way and going into great detail to make sure that this happens. The readers need to envision the scene in such a way that the action also looks credible; if you situate house A up-river from house B, a floating body which passes house B first will immediately worry your readers. Beyond the issue of credibility, however, it does not matter how readers see the scene; what matters is that they have a clear picture.

The picture you paint for your readers can be as full of allegorical devices as an Elizabethan portrait. The simplest words can be powerfully allusive. It would be difficult to suggest a family starving to death in a house with 'butter-yellow' walls. A white dress suggests innocence, white suits are for poseurs, white hair means old age and a white carpet means an urban interior which is cleaned every day by someone other than the occupier.

If you insist on giving something in your story an appearance which bucks your readers' associations – a twenty-year-old who is prematurely white-haired, a prostitute dressed in white – that contradictory picture must be presented with an acknowledgement and an explanation. Otherwise it will nag in the back of the reader's mind.

If you are taking your readers to a major location which they have probably never heard of, orienting them can become the business of an entire scene – the equivalent of that obligatory scene in World War II movies when the colonel gets out the map and points out the country, the river, the bridge too far and the enemy divisions.

Although visual information is vital and omitting it gives a story a peculiar feeling of being insubstantial or unstable, the noises, movements, smells and sensations of a location are also necessary to give the reader a really vivid sense of being there. And if the scene is viewed through the eyes of a particular character, his responses to it will also be part of the picture. A purely visual description is much less evocative, but easily produced if your own imagination is very visual, or if you have used pictures and drawings from your research to prompt your memory.

Here is the magnificently sensual introduction to the setting of Vicki Baum's *Grand Hotel*, seen through the eyes of Senf, the hall porter, who is stunned because he has just been told that his wife has gone into labour with their first baby:

The music from the tea-room in the new building beat in syncopation from mirror to mirror along the walls. It was dinner time and a smell of cooking was in the air, but behind the closed doors of the large dining room there was still silence and vacancy. The chef, Mattoni, was setting out his cold buffet in the small white room. The porter felt a strange weakness in his knees and he stopped a moment in the doorway, arrested by the bright gleams of the coloured lights behind the blocks of ice. In the corridor an electrician was kneeling on the floor, busied over some repair to the wires. Ever since they had these powerful lights to illuminate the frontage there had always been something going wrong with the overworked installation in the hotel. The porter pulled himself together and went back to his post. Little Georgi meanwhile had taken charge. Georgi was the son of the proprietor of a large hotel business who wanted to see his son work his way up from the ranks. Senf, feeling somewhat oppressed, made his way straight across the Lounge, where there was now a throng of movement. Here the jazz band from the tea-room encountered the violins from the Winter Garden, while mingled with them came the thin murmur of the illuminated fountain as it fell into the imitation Venetian basin, the ring of glasses on tables, the creaking of wicker chairs and, lastly, a soft rustle of the furs and silks in which women were moving to and fro. A cool March air came in gusts through the revolving doors whenever the page-boy passed guests in or out.

Re-orientation

Particularly at changes of scene it is important to reinforce earlier descriptions with a few words which call back the reader's image of the place. The device is the exact equivalent of the establishing shots used at scene changes in film or television drama – that quick shot of the car drawing up, the office immediately recognisable by its cluttered desk. The huge soaps of the Eighties, *Dallas* and *Dynasty*, used them so frequently that they became almost a code which regular viewers could read instantly.

In these re-orientation lines the writer can establish time passing as the scene changes according to the hour, season or year, and note the impact of the story's events on its environment. The dream kitchen can appear devastated after a party, the signs of bad husbandry can be noticed on a once-flourishing farm that has just changed ownership.

These passages also give the writer a chance to feed into the narrative the small details, such as reactions from walk-on characters, which will add to its strength. In *Grand Hotel*, the hall-porter is a walk-on character. His view of the hotel, the drama of the birth of his child, his conversations with the page-boy and the telephone operator, are a slender sub-plot which frames the main action of the story. The narrative returns to it occasionally, sometimes only for a few lines, reminding us of the expected baby, the revolving door, the reception desk and the telephone booths, giving a background picture of the hotel as an ants' nest of people who set aside their own dramas to toil anonymously for the comfort of the guests and the profit of the management. These scenes underline the larger theme of random meetings between strangers, and also give a sense of the hotel as a guest might experience it, coming in and out of the entrance, passing through the public rooms, dealing with staff whose faces gradually become familiar.

SUSPENSE

The basic technique of creating suspense is to arouse an expectation in your reader and then delay the fulfilment of that expectation. You leave them hanging – suspense.

When we read, our imagination is always racing ahead of the story, creating possibilities, testing them against what we know of the story so far, trying them out on the story-map in our unconscious and matching them to the accumulated expectations created by every story we have ever heard. Creating suspense is giving your reader's imagination plenty of time to chase its own tail in that process. Meanwhile, the need to know what happens next gets stronger and stronger.

How long should suspense be drawn out? As long as the need to know is growing; when it begins to peak it is time to bring the reader down, give them what they want, tell them what happens next. After the need to know has peaked is too late – the reader is bored and no longer cares. Too early, when the need to know is quite small, makes the readers feel cheated – they were looking forward to a long flirtation. In general, the more significant the next event, the longer you can spin out the suspense. Minor crises and small pieces of information need to appear reasonably soon after readers expect them, otherwise they will again feel cheated.

Cut to . . .

As soon as you introduce a new element into the plot, or send your character's life off in a new direction, or overturn the reader's perception of what's happening, you stop that story-line and cut to something else. This technique has already been discussed in the previous chapter. Here is an example from *Jurassic Park:*

> 'But you didn't get this graph,' Malcolm said. 'The graph you actually got is a graph of a breeding population. Your compys are breeding.'
>
> Wu shook his head. 'I don't see how.'
>
> 'They're breeding, and so are the othnielia, the maiasaurs, the hypsys – and the velociraptors.'
>
> 'Christ,' Muldoon said. 'There are raptors free in the park.'
>
> 'Well, it's not that bad,' Hammond said, looking at the screen. 'We have increases in just three categories – well, five categories. Very small increases in two of them . . .'
>
> 'What are you talking about?' Wu said, loudly. 'Don't you know what this means?'
>
> 'Of course I know what this means, Henry,' Hammond said. 'It means you screwed up.'
>
> 'Absolutely not.'
>
> 'You've got breeding dinosaurs out there, Henry.'
>
> 'But they're all female,' Wu said. 'It's impossible. There must be a mistake. And look at the numbers. A small increase in the big animals, the maiasaurs and the hypsys. And big increases in the number of small animals. It just doesn't make sense. It must be a mistake.'
>
> The radio clicked. 'Actually not,' Grant said. 'I think these numbers confirm that breeding is taking place. In seven different sites around the island.'

Cut to . . . the park, where there is a power blackout followed by a tyrannosaurus attack on the children – a massive diversion, but still not enough to make the reader forget the clear vision of the world being overrun by ferocious, carnivorous, intelligent, self-fertile and ever-multiplying raptors.

Withholding Information

This is a convention of the murder-mystery genre, the reason for the term 'whodunnit'. In that genre the information withheld is the killer's identity, which is not revealed until the end of the book. Any kind of story will be more enticing if you keep readers guessing by not telling them everything all at once. Withheld information makes people powerfully curious. Here is a double dose, from *Fatherland*.

> He turned his attention to the desk itself. A blotter. A heavy brass inkstand. A telephone. He stretched his hand towards it.
>
> It began to ring.
>
> His hand hung motionless. One ring. Two. Three. The stillness of the house magnified the sound; the dusty air vibrated. Four. Five. He flexed his fingers over the receiver. Six. Seven. He picked it up.
>
> 'Buhler?' The voice of an old man more dead than alive; a whisper from another world. 'Buhler? Speak to me. Who is that?'
>
> March said: 'A friend.'
>
> Pause. *Click.*
>
> Whoever it was had hung up. March replaced the receiver. Quickly, he began opening the desk drawers at random. A few pencils, some notepaper, a dictionary. He pulled the bottom drawers right out, one after the other, and put his hand into the space.
>
> There was nothing.
>
> There was something.
>
> At the very back, his fingers brushed against an object, small and smooth. He pulled it out. A small notebook bound in black leather, an eagle and a swastika in gold lettering on

the cover. He flicked through it. The Party diary for 1964. He
slipped it into his pocket and replaced the drawers.

Outside, Buhler's dog was going crazy . . .

What's in the diary? Thanks to the dog, we do not find out
until eleven pages later. And who was on the phone? Thirty-
three pages later we are allowed to figure that out for ourselves.
(Notice, by the way, how very filmic this passage is, how the
writer describes what happens exactly as a camera would see it,
and how the extremely short sentences and paragraphs enhance
the edgy feeling that the hero is trespassing in this house.)

What The Apaches Didn't Know

If your perspective as the storyteller is far enough away from
the action, you can give your readers vital information which
the characters do not have. Then the reader watches heart-in-
mouth as the character hurtles unknowingly towards destruction. In *The Thorn Birds*, the readers know from the second
month of her pregnancy, a little over halfway through the
book, that Meggie's son is the cardinal's child. She does not tell
him that until nearly thirty years later, after their son is dead,
almost at the end of the story.

All that time, the reader has been expecting that scene.
Throughout the second half of the book, there are so many
references to the boy's resemblance – physical, mental and
spiritual – to his father that the reader also expected the
archbishop to guess the truth at any moment.

Crank It Up

Reminding the readers where these landmines have been laid
in the plot increases their suspense still further. The basic
technique is a sequence of set-ups and pay-offs, of expectations
created and then fulfilled. The sequence should be more than
simply cutting away from the action and then returning to it,

or withholding information and then supplying it. Before you are ready to deliver the pay-off, you can crank up the suspense by reminding the readers that they are waiting, that they still don't know what is going to happen. Readers follow a powerful narrative with such deep concentration that a few words appearing after a hundred or more pages can be enough.

SHOCKS

The Heroic Journey leads the central character through a series of conflicts. At each encounter there is a danger that the hero will lose the battle and the reader, strongly identified with the hero, feels his fear. Indeed, in the most powerful stories he *doesn't* win them all: an early defeat makes the fear of losing all the more acute.

This series of conflicts generates a succession of emotional peaks and troughs which has a certain predictability about it. Moments of deep feeling which are not products of the conflict pattern counteract this effect. They add a rich counterpoint to the story and increase its emotional power.

The Bullet You Don't Hear

It's the bullet you don't hear that kills you. Surprise is the most powerful enhancement of suspense. Since you know the readers are trying to second-guess your story, you can start teasing them. Since they are listening for the bullet, fire a silent one. Play with their expectations. William Goldman advised, 'Give the audience what they want, but not the way they expect.'

Because the conflict pattern is predictable, readers need surprises to hold their interest. Every child knows that every fairy story will have a happy-ever-after ending. The real question in the reader's mind is not will the hero win in the end, but how. The writer must detach the readers from this cosy anticipation and suggest as strongly as possible that happy-ever-after will not come around unless the central character makes a supreme act of will.

Surprise gets the author a lot of respect. It reminds the readers that you're running the show, that you know what's going to happen and they don't. Like any other way of emphasising authority, it only works if it is used sparingly. Constantly surprising the reader is counterproductive.

Rebecca ends in a blaze of surprises – first the discovery that Maxim de Winter loathed his beautiful first wife, then his confession to killing her, and finally the revelation that she was in any case fatally ill. None of these is a predictable discovery, but all of them are hinted at long before they are revealed. The story is told so firmly from the viewpoint of the insecure, self-pitying second Mrs de Winter, that the reader ignores the clues just as she does.

Surprise must be used accurately, to confound the reader's expectation. What happens must be within the established characterisation, the plot structure and the laws of probability. Instead of the silent bullet, a wild surprise would be a hit-and-run driver. Wild surprises appear when the ground has not been prepared. They are not related to what the reader has antici-pated and so they undermine the author's credibility – a wild surprise is a small-scale *deus ex machina*.

Red herrings come under the heading of surprises. A red herring is a false trail, an anticlimax after a long period of suspense. You draw the reader's attention to something which turns out to be insignificant. The term comes from fox-hunting: a smoked, salted or dried herring, stained red to look more wholesome – in modern culinary language, a kipper – was dragged across the fox's trail and, being highly pungent, destroyed the fox's scent and confused the hounds.

Herrings in oceans occur in huge shoals; red herrings in books should occur singly and, if large, one per story is quite enough, unless you are writing in the detective genre, in which false trails are a convention. One or two small red herrings increase the reader's concentration and the writer's authority, but too many of them are an irritation.

Horror

Early in *Shogun*, a man is boiled to death. One of the group of Dutch sailors shipwrecked on the coast of Japan in 1600, he is killed for pleasure by the sadistic local ruler, who is to become a major antagonist. The ordeal lasts from sunset to sunrise. While the man's screams are heard all over the village, the lord enjoys the experience in a beautiful garden, composing poetry and watching the blossom petals fall, two courtesans in attendance. In the morning the 'shroud-covered, almost disjointed' body is ceremonially burned at the funeral ground.

This horrible event extends over twelve pages, although the description of the man in torment is accomplished in one short paragraph. Later in the book, an occasional reference to the 'Night of Screams' keeps the memory alive. Although nothing so macabre occurs again in the book, the reader is always afraid that it may. The torture vividly demonstrates that Japan is a terrifying, perilous and above all alien place for the central character, whose quest is for the understanding which ultimately ensures his survival.

Horror adds a powerful emotional charge to an event. Used in this way, at the start of a book it galvanises the readers' attention and maintains a level of fearful anticipation throughout the rest of the story. Ian Fleming often reserved brutal descriptions for the period of accelerating action leading to the climax, so that the horror intensified the readers' fears for the hero.

Episodes of horror are common in ancient mythology: 'It is a phenomenon found worldwide in myths and folklore . . . Psychologically, the brutal episode communicates an imperative psychic truth. This truth is so urgent – and yet so easy to disregard – that we are unlikely to heed the alarm if it is stated in lesser terms.'[1]

In a bestseller, also, horror must be used to a purpose. It gives an episode immense significance, and if this loading is not part

---

[1] Estes, op cit.

of the dynamic of the narrative, readers will experience it as gratuitous titillation. The implication that the author thinks they are reading just for cheap thrills is insulting (even if that is what *they* believe they are doing) and will sour their confidence in the author.

One man's cheap thrill is another man's total turn-off. The pitch of a horrific event must be geared to the conventions of the genre in which you are writing – if your book is in the horror genre gruesome episodes are mandatory, whereas in a pastoral romance it would probably be inappropriate to even see a cockroach, much less have the heroine crush it. When a man is burned to death in a bushfire in *The Thorn Birds* it happens offstage and we hear of it only in dialogue.

Death of a Loved One

The death of an attractive character is a severe shock. The reader expects antagonists to die, and the loss of a tedious minor character, like Beth in *Little Women*, is a matter of indifference, but someone who has become a friend in the course of the story is expected to be a permanent companion. Their death is not only a shock which adds a massive emotional weight to the story; if another character caused the death, the reader will hate them. If the central character grieves, the reader will grieve.

The archetypal model of this device is the death of Mercutio in *Romeo And Juliet*. Mercutio, forever joking, teasing and spinning fantastic stories, carries all the humour in the play. He is Romeo's dearest friend. He dies in a duel with Tybalt, Juliet's cousin and their arch-enemy, taking up Tybalt's challenge which Romeo has ignored. This event adds a huge emotional load to the narrative, weighting it towards the climax: Romeo at once kills Tybalt, thereby ensuring that his love for Juliet can only have a tragic outcome.

Ian Fleming often used the death of an attractive helper to do the same thing, to at last motivate James Bond against the villain. The deaths of Jill Masterson in *Goldfinger*, and Quarrel in *Dr No* are events which make destroying the enemy a personal imperative as well as a professional assignment.

Sex

Sexual events in a story produce very strong emotional reactions in the readers, who also have very definite sexual expectations of a book and of the characters encountered within it. Whether a love affair is the very stuff of the narrative or merely a counterpoint to it, readers expect a woman and a man who are attracted to each other to at least consider making love before the end of the book.

A very distinguished sexual psychologist once gave a lecture to a group of professional women in London. She had been the country's principal authority on sexual relationships for 25 years, and as I listened to her lecture I was struck by how acutely worried her patients had been by their sexual problems, often so worried that they could not function at all in the rest of their lives. With so much information about sex freely available, I found this strange.

When the time came for questions, I asked, 'Why do people get so worried about sex?' Before the psychologist could answer, women – clever, mature, successful women from many different professions – jumped up all over the hall, saying, 'People don't get worried about sex', 'Who says we're worried about sex?', 'Who gets worried about sex?', 'I'm not worried about sex', 'Sex doesn't worry me'. I had never heard so many women protest too much.

The point of this story is that the high emotional arousal which sexual descriptions create often feels like anxiety (think of the hideous fears let loose the first time you make love with a new partner). In a story the person who suffers most from this anxiety is the writer, which is why writing a sex scene feels so difficult.

If anxiety is the first problem in writing about sex, the second is detaching your writing from the legacy of pornography. For more than half the twentieth century sexual writing was banned

and literature, whether popular or literary, dealt with sex by
allusion. Thus marital rape could pass off like this:

> Somehow, her arms were around his neck and her lips
> trembling beneath his and they were going up, up into the
> darkness again, a darkness that was soft and swirling and
> all-enveloping.
> When she awoke the next morning, he was gone . . .
>
> GONE WITH THE WIND

In direct descriptive writing about sex, our inheritance from
the past is only pornography and a tiny collection of erotic
literature. These were works written specifically for excitement,
which do not address most of the emotional response to sexual
experience. They ignore most of what is now considered
normal sex, because in the past the majority of people's sexual
experiences were much more narrow and uniform than they
are now. Thirty years ago, for example, oral sex was considered
a perversion.

This means that most of what we have learned – consciously
or unconsciously – about sexual writing is of no use to us. The
words people commonly use in sexual description are still
considered dirty words. The language of sex has been colon-
ised by pornography, and so have many forms of sexual
experience. To write well about sex, it is necessary to go back
to your own instincts and feelings and work directly from them,
rejecting the influence of most of what you have previously
read.

The key to this is in the work of characterisation. A person's
sexuality is part of their character. Their sexual behaviour will
be determined by their self-confidence, physicality, kindness,
capacity for affection, courage, aggression, need for control and
need for emotional connection. In the character's backstory
their family attitudes and past experiences will also be
important.

If you allow a character to develop fully, sexuality and all,
their sexual actions will take shape naturally – not necessarily as
you would expect. One of my characters was a woman who

attracted an immense amount of sexual attention from men which she was happy to exploit for some years. Only as the book progressed and she began to form relationships, did it became clear that she was frigid: her sexuality had been traduced, she had lost touch with her own feelings and she was not going to form a full sexual relationship until she rejected that way of life.

More than any other major event in a story, the path towards a love scene needs to be prepared. Just as people in life get into the mood for sex, and enjoy that anticipation, so readers need to enter an erotic atmosphere quite slowly.

> They both smoked, saying nothing, drinking brandy, drinking coffee. A pheasant called from the fields. Jack, the collie, barked twice out in the yard. Mosquitoes tested the window screen near the table, and a single moth, circuitous of thought yet sure of instinct, was goaded by the sink light's possibilities.
>
> It was still hot, no breeze, some humidity now. Robert Kincaid was perspiring mildly, his top two shirt buttons undone. He was not looking at her directly, though she sensed his peripheral vision could find her, even as he seemed to stare out of the window. In the way he was turned, she could see the top of his chest through the open buttons of his shirt and small beads of moisture lying there upon his skin.
>
> THE BRIDGES OF MADISON COUNTY

Sexual description, more than any other kind of writing, benefits from being drafted, left to cool off for a while, then revised. It is at this stage that hackneyed words and pornographic clichés stand out clearly and can be rewritten.

The characters' emotions need to be present as well as their bodies; both characters' emotions, unless your whole story is told from one person's point of view only.

Since sexual relationships in a book have their own momentum, it is also important to balance their effect with the rest of the narrative. A love story in which sexuality is important ought to consider both the dark and light sides of experience, events which are boring, unpleasant, frightening or even traumatic as well as the moments of ecstasy.

> She kissed me. 'I love you,' she whispered.
> 'Darling, let's go to our lovely bed. I can see that look in your eyes – I like it.'
> And so we lay in bed. A man whose eyes could deceive a wife of nearly thirty years, and a wife who after nearly thirty years could be so deceived. Our practised movements were as pleasant as an old remembered song of long ago. But even as I surrendered to those final shudders, that are all and nothing, it was, I knew, a final defeat for Ingrid in a battle she did not know she waged. And it was a triumph for Anna, who had not even fought.
> I cannot and will not do this again. That was my last thought as Ingrid drifted dreamily to sleep in my arms.
>
> DAMAGE
> *Josephine Hart*

Repetition in sex scenes is a very easy mistake – one author who asked me for a read-through had four loss-of-virginity scenes and no more sex in 600 pages. It is also easy to include a sexual description at a point in the narrative which is logical from the point of view of the characters' feelings but not logical within the structure of the plot. One of my worst mistakes in *Pearls* was writing a beautiful love scene in the 26th chapter of a 29-chapter book. At this stage, close to the climax of the narrative, it is a distraction and most readers rush through it and forget it.

Reading a book is itself an act of intimacy. Between the writer and the readers a relationship of trust is created, in which the readers feel secure enough to open their feelings to the story. This is a vulnerable condition and the author can easily lose their readers' attention by offending them while they are in it. Readers' responses to sex are also highly subjective. Some are so sensitive that even a word like 'wet' is disturbing in a sexual context.

There is a widespread misconception among people who consider themselves above enjoying popular fiction that most women's bestsellers are full of gratuitous sex. Certainly, most women's bestsellers are about sexual relationships, which is not the case in popular fiction written for men. However, many of the most enduringly successful women's authors – including Danielle Steele, Barbara Taylor Bradford and Catherine Cookson – write love scenes which are almost devoid of explicit description. Sexual events which are not motivated by love do not occur in these books at all. The authors presume, correctly, that their readers have an extremely high sensitivity to sex and will be easily repelled.

REWARDS

Rewards are the treats which tempt the reader onwards. They are small details in the tapestry of the story which, if the reader notices them, will enhance their understanding. Giving your readers rewards for paying attention makes them more and more inclined to concentrate. Readers expect rewards and feel dissatisfied with a book which does not give them.

Because they help readers to anticipate the story and give them the opportunity to guess ahead of the action, rewards allow them the pleasure of feeling extremely clever. 'I *knew* that was going to happen,' says the reader who has been eagerly collecting rewards for six chapters.

Rewards also make readers feel comfortable in a book, which is to say that as well as feeling oriented they are also confident of your intentions towards them and full of anticipation of the delights to come.

The Broken Record

Repetition is a very simple way to reinforce the reader's memory. Repeating information is the basic technique of teaching, and if you want your readers to grasp something you must tell them more than once – but not in exactly the same words.

Repetition can reinforce character and motivation, as it does in *Fatherland:* early in the book, the hero puts on his SS uniform, which is described in detail. He looks in the mirror and doesn't like what he sees. When he goes out the people passing him in public places shrink away from him. As the story continues this fearful response to the black uniform, jackboots and swastika armband occasionally occurs again and is briefly noted. Whenever March can wear civilian clothes he feels relieved, human and happy. As well as describing his appearance, we are reminded of his discomfort in the role of a Nazi police officer.

This is significant information. Insignificant information can be repeated to re-establish time, place and character, but should not be emphasised to the point where the reader expects it to mean something.

Signposts

Readers don't expect you to waste their time. If you draw their attention to something by lavishing a disproportionate amount of detail on it, they expect you to be doing so for a reason.

The old knife was of iron, mottled with corrosion, its cutting edge honed down to a curve. The wooden handle was scarred with small burns and bound with packing thread where it had split towards the end. It was a vicious sturdy implement with a long career in the day-to-day butchery of the farm behind it. Jane had decreed that the knife had to be wiped, never washed, oiled if it was to be left unused for a while and kept in the lowest hole of the knife block . . .

She recalled her own advice and sharpened the knife against the carver, pleased that she could make the two blades flicker together in a fast, practised rhythm. 'A good mushroom knife must be exquisitely sharp, to cut the fungus

> cleanly, without any crushing.' Exquisitely sharp. 'Sharp
> enough to cut into the ball of your finger if you press it flat
> against the tip.'

The full introduction of the knife in *Harvest* extends over four paragraphs in the first chapter of the book. This gives the reader a very clear idea that this weapon is going to be fatal to somebody before the end of the story, and also hints at the huge reservoir of suppressed aggression in the character of Jane. A few pages later, when the knife is mislaid, the event is merely implied. Halfway through the book, over two lines, Jane cannot find it and we do not see it again until the killer's hand picks it up near the end.

Unless you are deliberately planting a red herring, do not draw excessive attention to something of no significance. Because your reader will expect anything which is emphasised to have a function in the plot, and they will feel cheated if you persuade them to pay attention to something which turns out to be unimportant.

Evocation

In a similar way, repeating the words or images which evoke an idea can make it echo through a book. This is appealing to the reader's instincts and feelings rather than the intellect, and so rather than producing a clear expectation of what is to come, evocation deepens the emotional tone of the story. *The Bridges of Madison County* is a web of evocations; there are several very brief references to Francesca as a young girl in Italy, implying that the innocent spirit of her younger self is being restored. There are frequent suggestions that Kincaid has mystical qualities, from his schoolboy assertion that IQ tests don't measure magic onwards. There are also hints, including his name and his appearance, that he is a displaced cowboy. Towards the end of the book the lovers either think or say these things, but by the time they are articulated in the text the reader has long held the same opinions.

A Soothsayer

A soothsayer is a person who tells the truth. You can hint at the developments to come by a few prophetic words of dialogue, placed so strategically that readers are bound to take note of them. In literature the archetypal soothsayer appears in Shakespeare's *Julius Caesar*, warning the emperor, 'Beware the Ides of March'. He takes the stage at the start of the play, at the very beginning of the second scene, immediately after Caesar himself makes his first entrance, and immediately before we hear the first murmurs of discontent from the conspirators who murder the emperor two acts later, on the day predicted.

A soothsayer can appear at any point in the story as long as enough emphasis is given to the prophecy. Apart from simply creating an expectation, they can also encourage readers to change their minds about a character or about the direction the narrative will take. I introduced a soothsayer in *Pearls* when a timid, feeble English planter's wife surprisingly begins to adapt to the terrible conditions in a Japanese prisoner-of-war camp. Her companion excuses her:

> She isn't strong enough to be unselfish. She can't do anything for herself in life, just survive, that's all.
> The older woman glanced down the length of the prison building, taking account of the sick and injured, the fretful children, the drawn faces and tattered clothes, the shins already blistered with tropical ulcers and the bones beginning to poke through dwindling flesh. 'That's all any of us can do – survive,' she said. 'I wouldn't be surprised if your friend turned out to be a great deal stronger than you imagine.'
> [The chapter ends here.]

Five years later this woman has survived, landed a rich and well-connected husband and sits spiderlike in the heart of her family developing passive aggression into a high art. Since the time-line of the story is doubled back, she is, in fact, already familiar to the readers in this role, but it is not until some time after this episode that her later identity is revealed.

Running Gags

Running gags are a convention in comedy, but could be used much more in other genres. Readers recognise them very quickly and, provided the device is not overworked, enjoy them more at every reprise. It is important that the joke develops at each reappearance, and ideal if it can be attached to a ramification of the plot.

> 'Splendid. That's it. Very good.' Nico nods; then some mercurial shadow passes across his face. I know him well enough to recognise that he has found a thought which he believes is to his advantage. 'I imagine Raymond's pressing pretty hard on that case.'
>
> 'Raymond Horgan presses pretty hard on every case. You know that.'
>
> 'Oh ho. I always thought you were the one who was non-political, Rusty. You're picking up your lines now from Raymond's copywriters.'
>
> 'Better than yours, Delay.' Nico acquired that nickname while we were both new deputy PAs working in the appellate section. Nico never could complete a brief on time. John White, the old chief deputy, called him 'Unavoidable Delay Guardia.'
>
> Presumed Innocent
Scott Turow

Nico Della Guardia's nickname, Delay, is used freely in the first part of *Presumed Innocent* as Rusty, the narrator and protagonist, makes clear his contempt for this ambitious, self-serving, camera-friendly lawyer, now his boss's major political opponent. Delay used to be his junior – he recalls firing him nine months earlier. He recalls annoying him while they tried their last case. He recalls all kinds of unflattering but amusing incidents in their mutual past – all of which becomes a tragic misjudgement at the start of the second part of the story, when Rusty is on trial for murder and Delay is the prosecuting attorney.

Unless you are writing a comic novel, there is probably only room for one running gag in your story, and although it can effectively feed into the main narrative, it should not be an integral part of it. Running gags are a diversion, light relief from the emotional demands of the story.

Comedy lightens the area around it, and running gags are almost a sign telling the readers that they can relax, that nothing major is going to happen for a paragraph or two. This is an expectation which can usefully be confounded; if something major does happen while the readers are chuckling, they'll get a hell of a shock and pay much closer attention to the story.

In John Grisham's *The Pelican Brief* the figure of the golf-crazed US President putting on the White House carpet appears as a running gag at first; only a bad poll rating can separate the President from his clubs. Later on he plays a few rounds with the Director of the CIA, his notion of an infallible loyalty test. The reader is lulled into regarding the President as a comic figure, until it begins to seem likely that half the action of the book has been engineered by him in a political conspiracy to cull his associates.

Because repetition always confers the expectation of significance, a strong running gag ought eventually to be drawn into the core narrative. Running gags are often carried by walk-on characters or in sub-plots, taking the stage during lulls in the action like the rude mechanicals in *A Midsummer Night's Dream*, before the final tangle with the main story.

Description

The total-structure school of fiction writing abominates description. This philosophy regards description as a block to the plot, something to be rationed to a lousy couple of lines in between the dialogue and the action. The goal is to be like

Ernest Hemingway, who instructed those who wanted to emulate his pared-to-the-bone novels to write first, then go back and cut out all the good stuff, and what's left is a story.

In my experience many readers do not share this sentiment. They like the good stuff. They luxuriate in descriptive passages and feel that a book is hardly a book without them.

Even the tautest texts from which I have quoted examples, like *Fatherland* and *King Rat*, include meaty descriptive passages, and because these descriptions make vital elements of the story elaborately and vividly real, they are the making of the books rather than their downfall.

At certain points your readers will not only like but actually need description, and there is every reason to give them what they want. Particularly in the middle section of the story, when you, the writer, are tiring, a well-fleshed description will revitalise both the story and your imagination. Another prime spot is just before the climax, when a description can function like the long flat run before the end of the roller-coaster, lulling the passengers into a false sense of security before the *coup de grâce*.

The one place in which extended description will weigh your story down is at the beginning, when the demands of establishing the scenario are already heavy. A pause for poetry here will not only add dead weight to the narrative, but it will irritate any structure freak in the book business who reads your manuscript.

7

What Every Story Needs

THE BEGINNING

The beginning of a book is its make-or-break zone. Apart from being the traditional place to start a story, the beginning is also the section of a book most read by people who are thinking about buying it, and the section of the book in which most people give up reading if the story does not give them what they expect. A book is judged on its beginning.

This is bad for the writer, who faces the awesome technical tasks of constructing a compelling start to the story and getting most of the major players on stage while still feeling their way into the narrative, the characters and the style of the book. More work probably goes into the first quarter of a book than into all the remainder.

The Best Strawberries

HILDY: (Shuffles through papers, then reads) 'While hundreds of Sheriff Hartman's paid gunmen stalked through Chicago shooting innocent bystanders, spreading their reign of terror, Earl Williams was lurking less than twenty yards from the Sheriff's office when . . .

WALTER: That's *lousy*! Aren't you going to mention the Examiner? Don't we take *any* credit?

HILDY: I'm putting that in the second paragraph . . .
WALTER: Who the hell's going to read the second paragraph?

THE FRONT PAGE
Ben Hecht and Charles MacArthur

The classic advice of the Canadian press baron Lord Beaverbrook to his journalists was: 'Put your best strawberries on top'. Newspaper writers learn early to put the most arresting fact of a story in the first paragraph. A book is far more complex, but it is still vital to seize the readers' attention on the first page, in the first paragraph – in the first line, if you can do it.

Deciding when and how to begin the story means choosing one of the best strawberries – a person, an event, an atmosphere, an idea – and putting it on top. Here are three brilliant beginnings which put three very different strawberries on top:

There are songs that come free from the blue-eyed grass, from the dust of a thousand country roads. This is one of them.

THE BRIDGES OF MADISON COUNTY

I'm going to get that bloody bastard if I die in the attempt.

KING RAT

The great fish moved silently through the night water, propelled by short sweeps of its crescent tail.

JAWS

Readers expect you to do this. They expect a confident assertion very early in the book that this is a story worth hearing. As well as issuing the invitation to the magic ground of the story, they expect you to get their attention, gain their confidence and hint at the scale of the mystery that is about to be unfolded.

Who Am I?

In the vast majority of the bestsellers from which I have quoted in this book, the central character appears on the first page.

One or two authors delay the introduction for a few pages – the longest delay is twelve pages. The need for the central character as an empathetic figure to carry the reader onwards is very strong and must not be frustrated. Without the central character, the reader has no vehicle with which to enter the world of the story.

Readers are like new-hatched ducklings, programmed to follow the first moving object that they see. If you introduce a vivid personality at the beginning of the story they will expect this to be the central character. An entrance ahead of the protagonist needs to be by somebody who quite clearly is *not* filling that role, like the judge who appears at the start of *The Pelican Brief* – 91 years old, paralysed, breathing bottled oxygen and expressing opinions which are intended to be obnoxious. Don't keep them on stage too long – the reader, still in search of the central character – will become impatient.

Where Am I?

At the very start of the book, the writer must give the readers the sign they are looking for, the confirmation that they are entering the magic ground discussed in Chapter Three (*see* p38). In the most compelling stories this is also done in the first paragraph, and certainly within the first two pages of the book. The sign can be any clear indication of this world's extraordinary dimensions – of the dangers, powers and emotions which will come into play later.

At the same time, the readers need to be oriented physically in the world of the story, so that they have an adequate understanding of the place, time and society into which they have ventured. Tempting as it is to do this with a huge scene-setting description, your story may commence more effectively if the necessary information is stripped in between actions. If you intend to set an urgent tone, to plunge your readers into a fast-flowing narrative and sweep them away, a substantial description in the first few pages will dam up the action and spoil the whole effect.

What's Going On Here?

Readers are very patient at the beginning of a story and willing to read for a while to get their bearings before events begin to move. How quickly you move the action forwards depends on the mood you want to create in this important period, and on the pace of the book. Action thrillers, which are typically highly dynamic linear narratives, often begin with a shock – a death, an explosion, a car crash. This proves to be the event which destroys the hero's world and compels the start of the Heroic Journey.

The aftermath of a death is a powerful place to begin, even if your genre is entirely domestic:

> My father has asked me to be the fourth corner at the Joy Luck Club. I am to replace my mother, whose seat at the mah jong table has been empty since she died two months ago. My father thinks she was killed by her own thoughts.
>
> 'She had a new idea inside her head,' said my father. 'But before it could come out of her mouth, the thought grew too big and burst. It must have been a very bad idea.'
>
> The doctor said she died of a cerebral aneurysm.
>
> THE JOY LUCK CLUB
> *Amy Tan*

On the surface, this is a book about cultural deracination, about four Chinese-American women separated emotionally from their mothers by the vast difference between the societies into which they were born. Notice how surely that idea is planted in the reader's mind at the very beginning of the book, in the contrast between the second paragraph and the first sentence of the third paragraph. At the deeper level, the lacquered, gilded, red-bannered Chinatown world is a safe place for us to feel the pain of growing up; here we can look into the gulf which each one of us has to open between ourselves and our parents in order to assume a separate identity. The image of a young woman taking her mother's place also evokes that theme.

Death is a traumatic event, but the death of a parent moves the child to the start of a new life passage. The particularly compelling quality of this beginning is that it makes clear what the psychological trajectory of the story is to be.

A story which is not going to move forward rapidly at the start can unroll at greater leisure, although there must be a strong hint of the action to come. Some authors choose to begin with the literary equivalent of a film's pre-title sequence, an arresting moment which may have been picked out from later in the story. There is great compulsion in beginning with a scene from the crisis area of the story which gives the readers a tantalising overview of the events to come. In a slower narrative, the beginning can cover the backstory of the central character, perhaps going back as far as their birth or beyond, although this is an extremely conventional approach.

The slowest beginnings are those in which the narrative is wrapped up in one or several other stories, where although the characters are introduced and the substance of the story indicated, there is a slow progression from the outer narrative to the core. This was a common device in films of the Thirties and Forties, and in nineteenth-century novels like *Wuthering Heights*, in which the story has been told to a narrator, who appears at the beginning to tell it again.

THE MIDDLE

The middle of the story is hard work. Writers who give up most often do so in the middle of a book, defeated by the demands of the monster they created with such ease in the first couple of chapters.

This section of a story is technically complex and motivationally arid. The thrill of beginning and the charm of creating your story's world have passed, the vision of the end is too distant to be inspiring. In addition, the middle of the story is where it can most easily go wrong. Holes appear in the flawless credibility of the scenario. Characters develop and refuse to behave in the way they should. Heroic figures become pathetic pygmies. The narrative plunges wilfully into blind alleys. Climaxes turn out to be melodramatic farces. Research is inadequate. Imagination fatigue sets in and the author gets miserable and depressed – sometimes to the point of quitting.

The middle of the story makes the greatest technical demands on the writer. It is here that the depth of your characterisation and strength of your construction will be tested, here that you need to work hardest to keep your readers' attention. This is where you have to get down on the mat with your ideas and wrestle them into something. Consequently, this is the part of the book in which your conscious mind is doing all the work. Things get very cerebral. The ideas stop coming.

Character Burn-Out

Halfway through writing *The Great Gatsby* the central character ran out of juice and turned into Scott Fitzgerald himself. As a result, even the author admitted that there is a void at the core of the story because Gatsby never really lives. The entire novel has a hollow feeling; the author considered it flawed, although in most people's judgement it is appropriate for Gatsby to be a hollow man since his way of life seems empty.

This is what happens when a writer loses confidence in their characterisation. You begin to fall back on your own reactions because your imagination is suddenly unable to tell you how the character which you have created would react. It may be simply a question of tiredness, or becoming bored with a story which you have been telling yourself for a long time – the condition I've called imagination fatigue and will discuss shortly (*see* p145).

There is a kind of character burn-out which is more than just a temporary failure of invention. This happens when you project yourself too far into a character – without realising what you are doing. The middle of the book, the period of trials in the heroic journey, will portray your central character being put through a series of tests, in the course of which she will be changing, moving into a new identity. When the character burns out, she is refusing to change; consciously, you want her to grow; unconsciously, you don't. Your character is fighting a battle which *you* are not ready for in real life; her journey of self-discovery is leading towards something which you yourself are not able to learn at this point.

This is not at all the same thing as recognising an aspect of the protagonist in yourself some time after the book is finished. Whether or not you understand your psychological sources during the writing process, the central character will never be yourself entirely, only a facet of you.

It may be possible for you to work out why your mind has unconsciously stalled your story; it may be quite obvious that there is something in your own autobiography which the action of the narrative has triggered in your memory. You may also be able to make the discovery with the help of a psychothera-pist. Until this inner wound has healed, you will meet the same wall again and again in your writing, but creative work itself is therapeutic and offers you the opportunity to conquer your own demon – as long as you have the courage to meet the challenge and not to quit the fight until it is over.

Whether you feel your difficulty is psychological, or merely a question of tiredness or boredom, the technique to remedy character burn-out in a story is to return to your original character structure. First read it through and fix the elements of the personality more firmly in your mind. You need to be totally sure now of who this person is. If you chose to leave the character as a simple sketch at the outset, now is the time to analyse their personality in more detail. If you decided not to bother with writing out their backstory – the story of their life before the start of the book – now would be a good time to do so. If you are using a visual reference, a photograph or a drawing, see if you can change it for fresh inspiration (I am not suggesting that you change the character's appearance, just find a new picture to help you think of the same face in a new way).

Take your character out to play. Depending on your tastes, there are all sorts of supplementary exercises you can do to help you see them as a rounded human creation. You can answer entertaining questions like: 'If this character was one of the

Magnificent Seven, which one would he be?' 'In a football team, which position would he play?' 'Would he cut the top off a boiled egg or bash it in?' 'If he won the lottery, what would he do with the money?' You could amuse yourself printing ink-blots and imagining the character's interpretations. You could complete a psychometric test for him or cast his horoscope. You could write his final school report or turn out his wallet in your mind and imagine the contents. Creation and playing are closely related processes, so a game can unlock ideas which will never be freed by serious effort.

The story should engage the protagonist to his limits, stretching him to find the strengths he did not know he had at the start. When you have a secure grasp of the character once more, go over the outline of the section where the burn-out took place and see if you pushed your protagonist hard enough. It is a common failing to let him off too lightly, to match him against unworthy opponents.

The reason is simple. Once again, *you* are living your story. Here in the middle of the book, when you are past the demands of scene-setting and introduction, it is easy to become totally involved in your own creation – in fact, most writers want to lose themselves in their stories and enjoy the blissful experience of events writing themselves. The problem is that in life a sensible person tries to avoid suffering, and in life the extreme things which happen in books rarely take place. When you start living your story it can suddenly become reduced in scale. The supernatural dimensions of the location vanish, the characters cease to be heroes and become mortal, the story is no longer an epic but a rather dull soap opera. It has dwindled to the size of life.

In this mundane scenario, the characters will be acting naturalistically because the only challenges they will meet are everyday problems. The writer needs to expand the story to its proper size again, and bring on antagonists of epic proportion. Instead of things happening to the protagonist which are merely bad, make sure that disasters happen to them. Do not be afraid to push them outside the original boundaries of their action – that is what the story must do to succeed.

Falling Out Of Love

You may have decided you don't like your central character. It happens. A story begins with a satisfyingly complex hero who embarks on adventures with enthusiasm; as more and more choices present themselves to him, the hero makes less and less defensible decisions. He seems to have no heart. There is a strong possibility that behind that satisfying complexity the man is just an asshole. Then the writer falls out of love with his hero.

This is an emergency. If you can't empathise with your central character, nobody else will be able to either. Do not try to solve this problem by superficial elaborations to the character; you may feel at this stage that his personality needs more human detail, but suddenly deciding that he plays basketball, supports his disabled sister or collects Jim Morrison memorabilia will not induce anyone to love him.

A common piece of advice for a writer whose protagonist appears unsympathetic is to 'make him suffer'. This is an oversimplification of the process. A reader who does not like a character will be quite happy to see him suffer. It is not suffering which the story needs in this situation, but a stronger response to suffering from the hero.

Go back to your original characterisation and focus on the central conflict between the cardinal and opposing qualities. See if you need to define these more strongly. The action of the story should on occasion reveal both these qualities at their extreme. Think about what will make your protagonist vulnerable – often a good or admirable quality, taken to excess, will be dangerous. Remember Nurse Nellie Forbush in *South Pacific* and her cock-eyed optimism? Cute as it was, that optimism made her foolish and gullible, vulnerable to exploitative lovers; to this day audiences sit through the musical with their fingers crossed, hoping against hope that the dear girl won't get her heart broken.

If you have fallen out of love with your protagonist, it may be that he is not extending himself fully as a character. His antagonists are big enough, the story has challenged him effectively, but he is responding in too small a way. The reader expects a more extreme reaction. If you make him act out more, and so deepen the characterisation through the action, he will at last start to develop engaging human dimensions.

Consider also your character's view of life and how it can best be expressed. By the middle of the book, your central character will have suffered, struggled and changed her opinion about a lot of things. The worm is beginning to turn. If she is still expressing neutral acceptance of her troubles, she will lose the sympathy of your readers, and lose sympathy with you. Some awareness is in order here, something to indicate that the character has noticed what is happening to her and is aware of herself changing. A little irony, a breath of cynicism, the occasional mordant one-liner might be in order. Humour always makes a character more popular, and in this situation it also indicates that she is getting control of her life again.

Unless you are writing a first-person narrative, your central character will not be able to make the ironic asides to the audience which can create a very strong bond with them. Characters may, however, make similar observations to each other.

> 'Now, Miss Elliott,' Brenda said, 'Did anyone ever tell you you're beautiful when you're angry?'
> Elise smiled at Brenda. 'No. Mostly they liked me passive. But those days are over, my friend.'
>
> THE FIRST WIVES' CLUB
> *Olivia Goldsmith*

Melodrama

Melodrama is under-motivation, advises Robert McKee. It is action on an epic scale for which the emotional context has not been supplied. If your story starts to become so full of pantomime violence that it reads like a scenario for a Punch and Judy show, you will find that you have skimped the motivational groundwork for the big scenes.

Go back in the text and begin to rebuild earlier scenes with this in mind. If the climax of the story is often foreshadowed in the very beginning of the book, the earlier conflicts which lead up to it can also be evoked over shorter time-lapses. This too is what your readers are expecting. They know that if an unpleasant figure appears in Chapter Three, by Chapter Eight they will be positively threatening and by Chapter Nineteen they will be an antagonist.

An important part of the contextualisation which creates drama rather than melodrama is the motivation of the antagonists. In emphasising the hero's motives for action, the opposing forces can risk being neglected. Negative characters have a tendency to be stunted and grow no larger than their function in the narrative. A person whose only purpose in a story is to be bad is a one-dimensional caricature. Especially if your story has a major villain, it is important to create vital and dynamic characters on both sides of the conflict. (Often, as in *Shogun*, *Fatherland* and *Goldfinger*, the one-dimensional, psychopathic villain is a minor character in the control of the major enemy, who is drawn with much greater depth.)

Imagination Fatigue

Bizarre as it may seem, a writer is never taught how to nurture the imagination. Writers are encouraged to analyse the imaginative work of other authors, but given no instructions for opening their own magic boxes. A vague injunction not to 'structure too much' or exercises which amount to literary variations on 'how many uses can you think of for a brick?' are the best we get, while down the hall in the visual arts faculty people are standing in front of easels learning a thousand different ways to bypass their conscious intelligence and let loose their creative instincts.

A user's manual for the imagination is the subject of another book (*The Artist's Way* by Julia Cameron is excellent and deals with blocks as well as self-development). In the middle of writing a story, what the writer needs are some emergency procedures to re-establish communication with the Muse when the lines suddenly go dead. There are ways to nourish the creative intelligence so that it stays robust enough to resist domination by the organisational faculties.

It is important to do this formally, allocating time and resources to imaginative regeneration, not just wandering off for a long walk and hoping it will get your head sorted. At times many artists will already use the techniques suggested here because they feel like the right thing to do; the difficulty comes in periods of extended effort, when you lose touch with the instinct that tells you something feels right. Nurturing your imagination means foreseeing those times, and following a work plan which will enable you to recover even when you can no longer recognise that you are in trouble.

Imaginative thought is pure creation. It originates from the right hemisphere of the brain, the centre of intuitive, holistic, non-rational and non-verbal thought, where constructing concepts is a process of matching similarities, perceiving patterns, synthesising ideas, employing metaphors, using feelings and images. Language is a left-brain function, related to logical, sequential, linear, rational, abstract and analytical ways of thinking.

How the two sides of the brain work together is currently a subject of widespread research. It is one of the major differences between men and women: women have substantially greater – 40% more – connection between the two hemispheres. In a man, the left brain works harder whatever the task given to the mind, while in women both sides will work even in a task which appears to be totally abstract.

Within genders, there are very wide variations in the way people use their minds. Even among writers, considered creative thinkers, there are people who favour their organisational side so much that their stories cannot move out of their own known worlds. These writers concentrate well, structure easily, and find characterisation an absolute chore, but since they do not rely on their imagination to write, a temporary failure there seldom disables them.

Highly imaginative writers, however, suffer more. I have known writers who are so instinctive that they can hardly order the words in a sentence. Their books are assembled from brilliant fragments. Their concentration is poor; what keeps them going is beguiling themselves with their own creation, and when they cannot do that they are in deep trouble.

There is another group in whom the connection between the two sides of the brain is so good that if a task involves mostly the abilities of one side, the other one also needs to be occupied. This condition – marked in my own family – is considered a minor dysfunction. It produces people who are dyslexic as children and who as students do their homework with the TV on. They work better with music and drive better with the radio. They are highly distractible, very observant, able to do two things at once, and exceptionally creative because they can articulate and structure ideas immediately. We are the last people to suffer imagination fatigue, but it comes to us at times, as it comes to every writer.

Writing a book means working with deep concentration for very long periods. The left brain begins to overwork and the right brain starts to shut down. It feels like a radio tuner wandering off a station. The transmissions get crackly, then start to lose volume, then fade to silence. To arrest this trend, the writer needs a work pattern which will allow the right brain recovery time:

✔ divide your writing time into periods of 45 minutes or one hour, and take a ten-minute break in between each period

✔ in that break, get up from your desk, leave the room and walk around. If your environment invites it, go outside and get some air. Take deep breaths or do a breathing exercise if you know how – you need to give your circulation a boost. Like any other bodily organ, your brain needs a good supply of oxygen to function at its best.

You're sure your brain is getting enough oxygen already? So was I, snug in my well-heated house on a crisp January morning.

Then I looked at my hands and saw that my fingertips were turning blue. *My* fingertips, served by my top-of-the-range, regularly serviced cardio-vascular system, pulse rate circa 60. No human body was designed to sit still for long periods.

✔ do not read or write in your breaks, and do not talk to people. Your aim is to throw the switch on your left brain, cut it out for a few moments.

✔ do something – one thing – to 'feed' your right brain.

Listen to music, but not highly structured pieces which will engage you intellectually – this is not a time to start picking out the themes in the *Ring* cycle. No comprehensible lyrics. You want something emotional – the soundtrack of *Paris Texas*, the meditation from *Thaïs*, Gregorian chant, Mahler, Tchaikovsky, Ligeti, Gorecki, Michael Nyman, the folk songs from the Auvergne.

Look at things, simple, pleasing things, especially natural forms – plants, shells, clouds. Take a quick shower, do a few exercises, go for a short walk. Be pretty aimless about doing these things; let your intuition guide you. You need a short period of reverie, a busy-doing-nothing break in which to tune back into your right brain.

✔ if you are practised and able to turn your thoughts away from your book, meditate for a few minutes.

✔ then go back to work.

In addition to these short recovery periods, give your imagination a long stretch of play time every day, at least an hour in which you are not engaged in any mental task and your mind is idling in neutral. For a lot of writers this is also an exercise period, in which they go for a walk, take the dog to the park, swim, run, cycle, play tennis, badminton or squash, do some yoga. Exercise gives you relaxation, a circulatory boost, an endorphin high, the nice smug feeling of meeting your aerobic goals and the reassurance that you are doing something to counteract the physical effects of a sedentary lifestyle, as well as time your mind needs to gather its intuitive strength.

Finally, be receptive to your thoughts at the times when the division between your conscious and unconscious minds is at its weakest – when you are waking up and going to sleep. These tend to be the disregarded borders of the day, periods which we do not think of as at all related to our work, but they are the times when the voice of the unconscious can be heard most clearly. Writers often report waking up knowing what to do about a problem that has been on their minds for weeks, or getting the answer in the last few seconds before going to sleep. These ideas can easily be forgotten when you are half awake, so keep pencil and paper by the bedside.

Writer's Block

Spit in the devil's eye – writer's block does not exist. It is a fancy name for one of four conditions – fear of failure, depression, post-traumatic stress or chronic imagination fatigue. Ways of dealing with the first two of these are discussed at greater length in Chapter Ten (*see* p195).

If you have reached the same point in this story at which you have given up before in previous books, you may be inheriting a specific fear of failure related to that experience. A psycho-therapist who specialises in treating artists has found that fantasies of failure are common among creative people: per-formers suffer from stagefright as a result, while painters and writers feel 'blocked'. The therapist uses cognitive therapy to combat this fear, putting his patients in touch with their own competence by asking them to remember their successes, and where there have been past failures helping them to notice the difference between those events and the present situation.

This is a technique you can use by yourself. Again, it is something which should be done formally, with time allocated in your schedule. Rather than merely remembering that you have accomplished things in the past, write down your successes and keep the list somewhere where you will see it as you work.

What successes? If this is your first book, you will not be able to remind yourself that you have written 500 pages before.

Perhaps you have done shorter pieces of writing which were received well – had an article or story published, a report commended. Perhaps you have also completed another kind of demanding task. Ten years before I wrote my first book, I made a patchwork quilt. It took three years and it proved to me for the first time in my life that I was persistent and could accomplish a long-term goal. I think of it – and get it out and put it on the bed and admire it – when I need to remind myself of that.

If your writing began well but suddenly ran into a wall, you may be facing an emotional trauma from earlier in your life, the memory of which can be completely suppressed. Unconsciously, however, your mind will be trying to heal itself, and so you have planned a scenario which addresses the area, instinctively seeking to work through the experience. When the old memory is recalled, however, your conscious mind still cannot deal with it and you have the feeling of complete mental paralysis. This may seem inexplicable – until a trained professional helps you to understand and overcome the problem.

If your writing degenerates into impossible struggle and you are reasonably sure that the reason is not trauma, depression or overmastering fear, the remaining diagnosis is chronic imagination fatigue and the cure a more ambitious programme of rest and recreation for your exhausted mental powers.

Chronic imagination fatigue is a last-resort diagnosis, but an easy one. When this condition has set in, life around you will be like the night of the living dead. You will have no conversation, no sense of humour and a short-term memory so overloaded you can hardly remember your own name. Without doubt you need to take a break now, but to stop yourself falling off the motivation wagon, plan a definite period of recovery time, minimum one day, maximum one week. This condition is the one acceptable reason for giving yourself time off from your writing schedule.

In your recovery period:

✔ get out of your writing environment

This is the perfect time to visit your old friends who have moved out to the country, or to jump into your car and drive until you run out of road. If you cannot get away from your home, at least get out of it for as long as you can. Leave your book and your writing implements behind. Your intention is not to think about the book in this period, although you may find your problems with it solving themselves once your intuitive faculties are restored.

✔ give your poor clapped-out brain simple, relaxing, repetitive tasks, anything which you find calming and absorbing – tidying cupboards, knitting, sewing, house-painting, clearing out a garage, ironing, cooking, stripping down an engine, digging a vegetable plot, rehanging roof tiles

As a young journalist, I was sent to interview Frederick Forsyth when *The Day of the Jackal* was filmed. His apartment was beautifully panelled with wood, and my eaglet eye noticed that the joinery was exceptionally intricate. When I commented on it, he told me that he had redecorated the entire apartment – panelling, painting and carpeting – doing the work to relax every day when he had finished writing.

✔ give your mind deep relaxation as well

Do anything which will put you in a meditative state – meditation itself, if you can, although at times of great mental stress it can be hard to switch off your conscious mind without more positive help. Watch the sea, from the shore or a boat. Go fishing. Take very long walks. Go running. Stay indoors and build a fire – even a candle flame is soothing to watch. Again, do not do these things in a structured, intentional way – 'now I'm going to spend two hours walking and at the end of it my mind is going to be back in shape.' You will not find the way out of this by looking for it. Let chance rule you for a while, be open to the experiences which come along, allow yourself to follow whatever lead your unconscious gives you.

✔ do not watch TV, read books, go to see films or plays

You will start relating everything to your book as your left brain reasserts its dominance over your thinking. Art galleries are fine, so is listening to music and watching dance, but keep these experiences as emotional as possible, try not to analyse the work. If you find these prohibitions too monastic, watch the simplest stuff you can bear, cartoons, Australian teenage soap operas or fluffy-puppy movies – you're trying to rest your mind, remember?

✔ do not talk about your problem more than you absolutely must

You will invest it with more power than it has already by talking about it. And you will start losing friends. In this condition only the most highly evolved souls can resist the temptation to pose Byronically around talking about the hell of being a writer. Coal-mining is probably hell. Night cleaner in an abattoir may be close to it. Writing is a privilege; your present difficulty will pass.

THE END

Even with the benefit of these restorative exercises, most writers reach the end of a book in a state of mental exhaustion – apart from the small number who begin planning with the end of the story and work backwards. For most of us, the task of drawing the narrative to a climax often does not receive the attention it deserves because by now the writer is beyond boredom and in a state much like that of the 38th week of a pregnancy – ready to do anything to get rid of the burden and back to normal life. Those who share the writer's life are fed up with living with a zombie, and friends are falling away since there is not much entertainment in a guest who is totally preoccupied and falls asleep at 9pm.

By this stage the book will have occupied so much of the writer's mind for so long that there may be no mental strength left to create the climax. With the entire book loaded into short-term memory – and some writers can recall the exact position of a single word in a manuscript of 200,000 words – the narrative may have strayed disastrously and be beyond calling back without extensive cutting. Planning the story at the outset will save you from these catastrophes. When your story is still a skeleton of events, you can ask yourself what is the last thing the readers will be expecting at the end and create one of those dazzling last-minute reversals which finish so many great novels. Three hundred pages later there may be no answer at all.

In theory, the end should write itself. It should be the logical outcome of what has gone before, and once the adventures of the middle section of the story are completed the narrative should accelerate towards the inevitable conclusion of the story. In practice, as you crawl towards the climax trying to remember what colour the heroine's eyes are, the forbidden god suddenly seems terribly attractive. Perhaps this is why, despite the fatal effect on a story, the *deus ex machina* ending still persists; it's just so damn easy. Much easier than setting up the final row of dominoes that will bring the game to an end. Fate *may* intervene in events; it does so with the death of Melanie Wilkes in *Gone With The Wind* (something the reader has expected since her first introduction as 'tiny and fraily built' and positively expected at any minute since she nearly died in childbirth halfway through the book), but an accident must not solve the hero's dilemma, only compound it.

A clearly defined structure is never so helpful as it is in drafting the end of the story. Overall, the conclusion will cover the final three events in the heroic journey – the mystical marriage, the supreme ordeal and the return – with a prelude and a period of resolution before the last battle which allow the reader space to prepare for the intense final experiences.

Prelude

The pace of the narrative should increase towards the end, particularly in an action story. Shorter scenes, with less description as the reader can now hold all the people and places in her memory, will increase the sense of urgency. If several story-lines are converging, the cutting from one to another can become so rapid that a couple of paragraphs will be all that is needed from each. This is a time to leave all decoration aside and allow the reader to look forward without distraction.

Whatever happens at the end of your story, it must take place because the hero makes it happen. As he approaches the final events of the narrative he will have changed, and at the beginning of the end – when the crisis, or mystical marriage phase of the heroic journey is imminent – he will become aware of his new self and be ready to assume the identity completely.

Often in this section of the story a major sub-plot is resolved. In *Shogun*, where the love affair between the English pilot and the Japanese noblewoman is the counterpoint to the pilot's struggles against a hostile warlord, the resolution of that relationship precedes the story's final events. Because the reader expects the climax of the story to use the whole stage, the ending of a substantial sub-plot also increases the sense of acceleration towards the finale.

Another common pattern at this point is the reprise of a part of the background story which will give the reader a piece of information which enables them to anticipate the ensuing crisis. This too adds huge impulsion to the final pages.

Crisis

This is the final turning point of the story, when the hero in his new self chooses a course of action which leads him to the last battle. Sometimes he has nothing left to lose at this point, sometimes he becomes convinced that his own life must be sacrificed to a greater good. This encounter will be the final test of his new consciousness, and it should be framed with the widest perspective the scale of your story permits – that is to say, the outcome should affect the character's whole existence in an intimate, emotional scenario, but if the story extends to social, national, global or universal levels, the outcome should have an impact in those areas as well. Once the crisis decision is taken, the reader knows what the end of the story ought to be – but not how it will come about.

In framing the crisis, remember that the readers will have expectations generated at the start of the story. If the heroine's inheritance is stolen by her sister at the beginning of the story, the readers will automatically expect a confrontation with the wicked sibling before the end. If her husband leaves her he will wish he hadn't. If the hero is unjustly fired, he will triumph over his old boss. If he set aside his first ambition to pursue his journey, the opportunity to realise it will be given to him – to reject from his new consciousness. Even if the character who wronged the hero is dead by the conclusion, there will still be a strong expectation of some form of confrontation between the two of them – through the will, a newly discovered letter or the testimony of another person.

Resolution

Your readers will also feel a degree of exhaustion at this point. With the central character, they have made a long and dangerous journey. The climax of the book will make final emotional demands on them, and a period of resolution will allow them to gather their strength as well as increasing the feeling of suspense to the maximum.

The end of the story is a very prominent position and anything placed here must either build towards the climax or be a distraction which will be enjoyed only because it is part of the final dynamic structure. The readers are gasping for the final scenes and will simply skip anything thrown in their path now unless they understand its purpose instantly.

In the resolution period, minor sub-plots can be resolved – one by one the mysteries of your story are revealed, leaving the greatest of all until last. You can also tie up any remaining questions in the backstory, although placing a revelation in this exalted position demands that it be nothing less than the one missing piece in the deductive jigsaw of the plot. It should be showcased with all the skill you have, to counterbalance the anticipated impact of the climax. The shock tactics described in Chapter Six (*see* p111) could be useful here.

Fresh elements can revitalise the text at this point, as long as they are not laboured. At the end of *Pearls* the resolution passage is a backstory excursion which fills in the events in the life of the heroine's father leading up to his suicide, some of which take place at Longchamp racecourse while the Prix de L'Arc de Triomphe is running. I was exhausted by this stage in the writing but the pleasure of describing the scene, and of discovering, through a helpful racing journalist, that the race is archived in conscientious detail every year, gave me renewed energy which breathed new life into the characters and created a new twist to the plot. However, a scene which lasts three pages here parallels a passage near the start of the book which extends over seven.

The pace of the narrative, which will have accelerated to this point, can be relaxed to give the reader a period of calm before the storm. However, it is important not to make any big demands on the reader here, not to introduce a new character or a concept which requires a real mental effort to understand. Long descriptions do not belong here. Humour does not usually sit comfortably. The audience is tired and impatient. Charm them by all means, beguile them for a few pages, startle them because they need to be kept alert, but do not bore them or they will get angry.

The Climax

In this long-awaited scene the hero stands before us in the full strength of his new identity, whole, healed, wise, strong and triumphant. But not necessarily either happy or successful. When you are considering how to end your story, remember that it is the *inner* journey of the hero which is really important, not the external one. We know that in life self-discovery has to be its own reward, and so in a story the most satisfying ending is rarely the standard happy-ever-after thing.

Certain genres have conventions governing endings. In murder stories, the killer must be discovered. In romances, the woman always gets her man. In vampire tales, the undead gets the stake through the heart. There can be some surprise attached to the identity of these parties, but the event itself is required to take place.

The pace of the narrative will pick up dramatically now and the climax often carries the least flesh of the whole story. There is no place at all for extended descriptions, and the re-orienting phrases which were needed earlier in the narrative should be abandoned now. The book will be concentrated into one story-line, one character and the one event which will finally demonstrate the theme of the work. There may or may not be an antagonist on stage in this last scene – sometimes the climax is an internal battle, sometimes a struggle with a whole institution or all of society itself.

The challenge of the ending is to create power without bulk, to write simply but with tremendous force. The emotions of the central character are a key factor in achieving this. The reader has lived the whole story on an emotional plane and is seeking a peak experience at the end, a catharsis, a complete discharge of the immense feelings which the narrative has aroused.

There are many techniques which emphasise the emotional content of an ending. In *Fatherland* the text, which has until now made rare and brief excursions into the hero's internal world, suddenly moves right inside his imagination, projecting his desperate hopes onto the page in between the last moments of action. Conversely, in *Jaws* (which as a book is an emotional story to which the menace of the shark is only background) the violent action of the hunt comes at the end, giving the hero a way to act out what he feels. In *Presumed Innocent* an emotional plot encloses the murder mystery; the personalities of the central character's wife and of his murdered lover are both enigmatic until the closing scenes, when the deep feelings of both women are suddenly made clear.

The Final Curtain

After the climactic scene or scenes, what remains is to bring your readers down from that peak experience and help them to recompose themselves. They should by now be feeling vulnerable but profoundly satisfied. Your story has explored one of the great caravan roads to wisdom, a path which is unmarked although millions have taken it. You have been their guide on a journey into the unknown, and now it is time to say goodbye.

You may have decided on an enigmatic ending. What happens in the world after the hero's journey is complete can be imagined by your audience, because of the mythic nature of a story. They can extrapolate the effects of the climax from a few words. It is necessary only to hint at the final outcome, but it is necessary to give that hint, the essential reassurance that things do end as anticipated.

Conclusions which are tragic or negative in other ways – suggesting that there is no hope for characters or situations – need to be mitigated. Only in an opera can the lover die, the heroine kill herself and the curtain run down immediately. The audience can handle their shock by exchanging knowledgeable criticism of the tenor's voice and strolling away to dinner. At the end of a book your audience is one person, alone with turbulent feelings, perhaps at 3am, who will appreciate a gently managed re-entry into the actual world. Shakespearean tragedies make good use of figures like Horatio in *Hamlet* and the Prince of Verona in *Romeo and Juliet* who take the stage in front of a pile of corpses to speak kindly of the dead and connect the tragedy to the larger concerns of its society. Raymond Chandler lets Philip Marlowe get a little Shakespearean at times:

> I'm not saying she was a saint or even a half-way nice girl. Not ever. She wouldn't kill herself until she was cornered. But what she did, and the way she did it, kept her from coming back here for trial. Think that over. And who would

that trial hurt most? Who would be least able to bear it? And win, lose or draw, who would pay the biggest price for the show? An old man who had loved not wisely, but too well.

FAREWELL, MY LOVELY

If you have created engaging minor characters, the readers will want to know how their stories end, and in a book – although very seldom in drama – the conclusion of a sub-plot can make a graceful ending. It is tempting to conclude an elaborately textured story with a long wrap-up passage explaining the fate of every single character in the story. Unless you can formalise it wittily, this will probably not be read. The majority of your minor characters need to have their destinies settled before the climax; afterwards, the sub-plot to resolve is the one which most powerfully underlines the theme of the story.

In the final few pages of the book you can also call back minor characters to comment on the action. Particularly after an outright happy ending, this is a good place for humour, although only a strong joke can carry the ending of a book. A well-developed running gag can make its final appearance. This is also a wonderful position for an image:

Below the bows of the Arrawa a child's coffin moved on to the night stream. Its paper flowers were shaken loose by the wash of a landing-craft carrying sailors from the American cruiser. The flowers formed a wavering garland around the coffin as it began its long journey to the estuary of the Yangtze, only to be swept back by the incoming tide among the quays and mud-flats, driven once again to the shores of this terrible city.

THE EMPIRE OF THE SUN
J G Ballard

CHAPTER

8

Casting

In one sense you are never alone in a book. People are the whole story, everything you write about is a human action, perception or feeling. Whatever you describe will be seen through the eyes of one of the people you have created. Whatever you think will be explained by them. Who you choose to act out your drama and how you portray them are not only highly significant choices but probably also the most enjoyable ones in the entire process.

The Principals

The heart of a story only has room for two or three characters – perhaps the hero, the guide and the threshold guardian, perhaps the hero, the lover and the major antagonist. Only if there is more than one central character, and more than one story-line, will the essential core of the narrative be populated by more than three people at a time. With multiple story-lines, or books spanning several generations, the principals will change.

The people who are to share the spotlight with the central character need to appear equally powerful, while the supporting cast and the walk-on parts will blend into the general background and are therefore drawn with less depth and detail. The seven-question analysis detailed in Chapter Three (*see* p52) can be used as an aid to imagining these primary characters as fully as possible.

The core of the story will be enacted by this small team and they need to be distinct and complementary personalities in every detail. At the deepest level the guide will supply the knowledge which the hero lacks, the threshold guardian will have the conformist qualities which he rejects, and the enemy will uphold an opposing value system, but at the surface they will also be contrasted in terms of age, nationality, appearance and temperament. Their names, in particular, must be completely unlike each other: if you juxtapose a Maria and a Marina, or a Johann and a Jonathan, the reader, following the narrative against distraction, will be confused.

Unless you are writing a first-person story, or have decided to restrict yourself only to the central character's perception of events, you will at times write from the point of view of each of the principals. Most of the story will be told from the protagonist's viewpoint, but to reach its full emotional range the thoughts and feelings of all the main players need to be added to the picture – especially at moments when their emotions are running high.

When two characters are companions for much of the story, reacting to events together, it is useful to think of them as a duality, two people who have the same beliefs but act on them in completely different ways. Diaghilev described two dancers as being like two halves of an apple, although only one had ripened in the sun. In *Fatherland* the hero and his threshold guardian, both police officers, are nicknamed the Fox and the Bear, which tells you everything essential about their temperaments. Added to this central duality is the lover, a young American woman whose freedom from Nazi indoctrination facilitates the final liberation of the hero's will; these three are drawn in equal detail, with the minor and major antagonists from the SS added as powerful but less lifelike figures.

There is no obligation to make the protagonist the most charismatic character in the story. In *King Rat*, the King of the title is a guide figure, the sussed, street-wise American corporal from whom the hero, a British officer, learns not merely to survive the Japanese prisoner-of-war camp but to thrive there. The King dominates the story; the supporting characters are obsessed with him, and although the reader is frequently invited to question his morality, he is the real star of the show. He is bold, ignorant, amoral, muscular, American and an enlisted man, while the true protagonist, Marlow, is reserved, educated, principled, scrawny, British and an officer. Against them is another Briton, Lieutenant Grey, beside whose bitter sadism the Japanese commandant appears as only a minor enemy.

An author seldom has trouble making a villain and a hero different, but it is never enough to depict the major antagonist as just a person who is bad because that's the way they are. Villains are people too, with their own inner tensions and fundamental contradictions. However evil they are in the final judgement of the world, they themselves believe they are doing the right thing. You should be able to understand them, to argue the case from their side, to pity them and even to love them at times. If you reduce them to little more than their role as bad guys the whole balance of the story will suffer.

Goldfinger, one of the most memorable villains in popular culture, is by far the most fleshed-out character in the book of the same name (although since James Bond is already known to us he does not need the same detailed establishment). He is presented with such vivid sympathy that we overlook his repellent superficial characteristics and become absolutely intrigued.

Goldfinger appears first as a ridiculous but arresting image, a man in yellow satin bikini trunks sunbathing with a metal reflector to tan the underneath of his chin. He is slightly deaf and calls our hero 'Mr Bomb'. Nevertheless, he is immediately fascinating to Bond, and to us:

Mr Goldfinger was one of the most relaxed men Bond had ever met. It showed in the economy of his movement, of his speech, of his expressions. Mr Goldfinger wasted no effort, yet there was something coiled, compressed, in the immobility of the man.

When he had stood up, the first thing that had struck Bond

was that everything was out of proportion. Goldfinger was short, not more than five feet tall, and on top of the thick body and blunt peasant legs was set almost directly into the shoulders a huge and it seemed almost exactly round head. It was as if Goldfinger had been put together with bits of other people's bodies. Nothing seemed to belong. Perhaps, Bond thought, it was to conceal his ugliness that Goldfinger made such a fetish of sunburn. Without the red-brown camouflage the pale body would be grotesque. The face, and the cliff of crew-cut carroty hair, was as startling, without being as ugly, as the body. It was moon-shaped without being moon-like. The forehead was fine and high, and the thin sandy brows were level above the large light-blue eyes fringed with pale lashes . . .

It was the short men that caused all the trouble in the world. And what about a misshapen short man with red hair and a bizarre face? That might add up to a really formidable misfit. One could certainly feel the repressions. There was a powerhouse of vitality humming in the man that suggested that if one stuck an electric bulb into Goldfinger's mouth it would light up . . . What had he been born? Not a Jew, though there might be Jewish blood in him. Not a Latin or anything farther south. Not a Slav. Perhaps a German – no, a Balt! That's where he would have come from. One of the old Baltic provinces. Probably got away to escape the Russians. Goldfinger would have been warned – or his parents had smelled trouble and they had got him out in time. And what had happened then? How had he worked his way up to being one of the richest men in the world? One day it might be interesting to find out. For the time being it would be enough to find out how he won at cards.

In novels which form a series with the same central character – James Bond, Flashman, Angelique, Inspector Morse – the author needs only to touch base with the personality occasionally. Usually the first book in the series establishes the character in detail and the subsequent stories assume that the reader understands them. It is unusual for such a character to change and grow, the reader's pleasure in such a series is often in their consistency, although Angelique matures from a naive girl to a worldly woman, with intervening descents into bitterness and decadence, over the first five stories in the cycle.

Supporting Roles

Fascinating as people are, you cannot invite anyone into your book unless you have a job for them. The medium-weight roles in your story belong to characters who are vital working components in the mechanism of the plot but who are not part of its core. They are essential in the web of the narrative, and their characterisation also supports that of the principals, either by contrast or agreement.

There are certain characters who at first may not have an obvious function in the narrative but whose presence is demanded by the natural curiosity of the reader. In an emotional story, readers will wonder about the earlier lovers or friends. If the principals are old enough, their ex-husbands or ex-wives may be part of their portraits, their children too.

The protagonist's family of origin is obligatory, but it is not necessary to bring them on stage. An indication of the relationships with mother, father or siblings is a vital layer in any character. Their attitudes to the protagonist and his or her way of life are extremely important.

Mitch, the central character of *The Firm*, passes his relatives almost as milestones on his journey towards himself. It is clear from the very beginning of the book that the law firm which recruits him has sinister aspects; we need to know why this brilliant graduate focuses only on their high salary and seems undisturbed by their fascist business practices. The book indicates, through Mitch's relatives, the sense of inadequacy which lies behind his apparent ambition to be nothing more than a 22-carat yuppie, and the lack of guidance with which he and his young wife are setting out in the world.

First he confronts his in-laws, the small-town bourgeois creeps who boycotted his wedding, whose hostile materialism alone might have pushed him from beyond plain ambition to fatal greed. Then he visits his brother, who is to play a part in the story later but is encountered first in jail for killing a man in a bar-room fight; the two of them 'could pass for twins' and the brother looks up to him for being the first of their family ever to amount to anything. We learn that his father died when the boys were young after which his mother was committed to a mental hospital. Finally, on Christmas Day, Mitch sends his wife off to visit her parents alone and heads to Panama City. He calls a cab at 11pm and tells the driver to take him to the Waffle Hut, where he waits outside. He watches the frail, grey-haired waitress, on her feet, taking orders and smiling into the early hours of Christmas morning. This is his mother. He watches her for a while, then drives back to his hotel without making contact, apparently unable to bridge the gulf that his own ambition has opened between them.

Walk-on Parts

Even the most minor characters need a role in the story, but they do not need a close relationship with the principals. In this league you can bring on characters whose entertainment value exceeds their actual function. The most minor characters can be the most colourful, because they are only present in the story for a short time; like hummingbirds, they dart into the scene, dazzle for an instant, then disappear.

Such characters need a function in the narrative, however small, but their great value is as part of the story's location, which their behaviour can bring alive far more vividly than plain description. They are ramifications of the 'don't tell me, show me' principle. In *White Ice* a young American runs off to the south of France to find his Russian grandmother, once a famous dancer but now living in a community of decrepit ex-patriates in the suburbs of Nice. To communicate, they need a translator:

Another old woman appeared from the villa opposite, shriek-ing in response, a small brown dog with bulbous eyes at her feet. The two women called to each other like parrots over the straggling purple bougainvillaea, then gathered their skirts around their knees and returned indoors.

Some time later a voice called, 'Yoo-hoo, yoo-hoo!' in the front garden and the knocker on the front door, a useless nickel-plated ring, was flapped impatiently. Marie set off and returned with their neighbour, who extended to Alex her translucent, freckled hand, its fingers swept sideways by rheumatoid arthritis.

'Good *after*noon, young man. I am Angela Partridge and as you can probably hear I am English.' She was wearing a pleated silk afternoon dress in some beige print that looked like scribbling, with pale support stockings most carefully darned. The dog sat down at her feet and raised one forepaw. 'And this is Sir Horace, he is a griffon and he would like you to shake his paw. That's right.'

'He's got a cute face.' Alex noticed how clean the newcomer seemed beside the others and how the fresh air admitted by Marie's exit was still hanging in a cloud in the centre of the room.

. . . 'Since I speak something like your language, your grandmother – I believe it is – has invited me to translate, so I shall do my best. I do hope your journey was not too tiring.' She seated herself on a hard dining chair, turning round to ascertain its condition first. 'Did you fly? Simply thrilling! Do tell me – how long does it take?'

White Ice

Introduction and Revelation

My own novels are richly textured and heavily populated. Angela Partridge, a walk-on part, is more elaborately realised than the central characters in those novels whose style is spare and pared to essentials. In genres such as action or comedy the formal characterisation will be a matter of a few sentences plus a few telling details like a nickname or a nagging doubt. The character's actions, their behaviour, their choices, their decisions, will then tell the reader all they need to know.

It is not necessary to define every detail of a fictional personality – in fact, it may be more effective not to do so because a figure which is only sketched offers the reader more scope for identification. Such characters are almost like blank screens onto which readers project their own images. The more you particularise a personality, the greater the risk that your reader will say, 'Oh, that's not me,' and start to pull out of the story.

While the central character is usually introduced fully at once, it is extremely compelling for other major characters to reveal themselves slowly:

'You are Martyn's father. I'm Anna Barton, and I felt I ought to introduce myself.'

The woman who stood before me was tall, pale, with short black wavy hair swept off her face. She was a figure in a black suit and smiled not at all.

'Hello, I'm so glad to meet you. I seem to have missed you each time you've been to the house.'

'I've only been there three times. You're a busy man.'

It should have sounded abrupt, but it didn't.

'How long have you known Martyn?'

'Not very long.'

'Oh. I see.'

'We've been . . .' she hesitated, 'close for about three or four months. I knew him a little before, through work. I work on the same paper.'

'Oh, yes. I thought I recognised your name when I first heard it.' We stood silently, I looked away. I looked back. Grey eyes stared straight back into mine, and held them and me, motionless. After a long time she said:

'How very strange.'

'Yes,' I said.

'I'm going now.'

'Goodbye,' I said.

She turned, and walked away. Her tall black-suited body

seemed to carve its way through the crowded room and
disappeared.

DAMAGE
Josephine Hart

The reader has already had an indication that the woman this
man's son is courting will be significant in the story. This
introduction, with its high tension, spare description and
deliberately banal dialogue, makes her appear a disturbing
enigma. No unsmiling woman in a black suit is likely to be on
the side of the angels, but the lack of detail is utterly tantalising.
While her character is explored obsessively as the story continues, the full depth of her mystery is not sounded until the
very end of the book. Much of the story's impulsion is created
in the impression that there is a toxic secret somewhere in a
locked room in her heart; in the final revelation she is as evil as
the reader has already imagined her to be.

As a story progresses, the author can reveal more and more
of a character, but must also remind the reader of their basic
qualities at each appearance. To survive this process, the
character needs the sound basic architecture already discussed.
The writer needs to imagine the character holistically, then
select telling details from the picture as they are needed.

Readers understand a character primarily through what they
do, how they look and what they say, but added to those main
areas are the little things which mean a lot. You can think about
a thousand external expressions of a personality: how they
sound, their tones of voice; how they smell; their mannerisms
and habits; how they move, how quick, or supple, or agile they
are; how they would open a car door, sit on a chair, cut a piece
of bread; what their energy levels are, what tires them, what
galvanises them; how – or if – they would vote; how – or if –
they like coffee.

For principals, as Ian Fleming did for Goldfinger, you should
also consider what screenwriters call their backstory, all the
events of their lives before they meet the reader for the first
time. This history is helpful for you to imagine in detail,
but may not appear in the book as more than a few hints.

The family relationships are important, and beyond that the cultural background – is this a native, a first-or-second generation immigrant, a foreigner, a northerner, a southerner, an urban cowboy, a country girl or a nerd from the 'burbs? How well were they educated, and by whom? A very important question is their religious background, since whatever their personal morality may be it will have formed in reaction to the moral culture in which they were raised, be that anywhere between crack-dealing atheism and Exclusive Brethren.

Psychology

Psychology is a discipline which a writer can use to analyse ideas, but not a means of creating a character. If you know the cast of your story the way you know living people – whole and usually beyond rational explanation, however much people chew each other over *in absentia* – you will be able to get them down on the page in a form which will seem lifelike to everyone. If you start tagging your people as 'passive-aggressive' or 'a phallic narcissist' you will rapidly bleed all the vitality out of your story.

'How would you describe a phallic narcissist?' I asked a therapist friend. 'A total prick,' she replied. Psychiatry tends to think of people in terms of problems. This is a fundamentally judgemental view of the human condition which is no help to an artist who wants to create a functioning character. If you intend to explore a personality which is unquestionably psychotic, the psychological consensus about their condition is something which must be considered because it will have formed your readers' expectations. In general, however, a writer needs to think of people positively; as you are writing your principal characters you will almost enter their skin and become each of them in turn.

Self-help psychology is even less useful than the full-dress kind. In a self-help book everybody is wrong, somebody more than the rest (that'll be you, the fool who bought the book) but

– phew! – this nifty ten-point plan will set you straight and help you reclaim your life.

Self-help psychology acts on stories like the Ebola virus on people – death is rapid and inevitable. It's fatal to lyrical scenarios; conceiving Kincaid as a typical commitment-phobic male would not have created *The Bridges of Madison County*. It's fatal to adventure: if Isaak Dinesen had read *Smart Women, Foolish Choices* she would never have got out of Denmark, much less *Out of Africa*. It's fatal to action: if James Bond followed the seven habits of highly effective people he would have stayed home with M, polished up the mission statement and empowered Miss Moneypenny with the old licence to kill.

The fact is that to a psychologist all heroes are dysfunctional. Getting the love you need is incompatible with the heroic journey. The authors concerned in both fiction and non-fiction sections want the same thing – the spiritual growth of their readers – but they go about it by processes which are totally incompatible.

Guest Appearances

A cameo appearance by a famous person from the real world is a favourite exercise of both literary and popular writers. Judith Krantz, recreating the Paris art community of the 1920s for *Mistral's Daughter*, had excellent fun with Picasso, Matisse, Chagall, Cocteau and Scott Fitzgerald among the extras when the *Bal Sans Raison d'Etre* degenerated into a pitched battle between the Surrealists and Realists.

Entertaining as real people can be in a novel, they need to be treated exactly as if they were completely fictional. They need to be introduced, established and characterised as if none of your readers had ever heard of them. Parking a real person among imagined characters like a Mount Rushmore face – huge, silent and dominating – is a blow to the credibility of the story and the authority of the author.

It is useful to approach the god-like one from the perspective of their feet of clay. In *White Ice*, Anna Pavlova, Vaslav Nijinsky and the other members of Diaghilev's Ballets Russes make frequent appearances. Although the judgement of history is that these were the greatest dancers of their time, many of their colleagues never held such an opinion. Half St Petersburg society considered Diaghilev a flaky degenerate who never paid his bills, while at ballet school Nijinsky was a stupid Polish boy who could jump but was more than a little weird. Nor was the pre-legendary Pavlova universally admired, as this conversation between two junior ballerinas and a would-be choreographer makes clear:

> For a while they walked on slowly in silence until Leo could not bear any more. 'So, what do you think of my idea, Lydia? Don't you think it's good?'
>
> 'You asked Anna to dance the pas de deux.' At last she turned around, but her stony face shocked him. 'So much for your admiration for *my* dancing.'
>
> 'Oh Lydia, don't be hurt. You can see how things are with her and Dandre, and he's the boss after all. Believe me, I'd a thousand times rather create something marvellous for you than have to beat my brains out finding something she can do with those pitiful knees of hers.'
>
> 'I just hope she falls into the prompter's box again, that's all. That'll teach you to respect a real dancer.' She folded her arms crossly and accelerated away from him.
>
> 'Please, Lydushka, I can't do anything else. And maybe it will work out, you know. I know Sergei Pavlovich wants Anna for his Paris season if it comes off.'
>
> Lydia gasped, momentarily winded by multiple jealousies. 'Paris! Oh, it's not fair. Why should Anna be going to Paris when she hates fun and parties and clothes and having a good time and she's a prig and a bore and a cripple and she only gets decent reviews because she sleeps with the critics . . .' In the glow of the street lamp her eyes were so bright and full it seemed as if she were about to cry.

Marie hugged her briskly. 'Lulu, darling – only one critic, you be fair now.'

'Well, one was enough.'

WHITE ICE

Dialogue

Your people will come alive in their own words. Dialogue is speech which is used to illuminate the developments of the story, either by giving information or expressing attitudes. Good dialogue sounds natural, but in fact is highly edited and condensed in comparison with the way people actually speak.

Dialogue is one of the most important elements in characterisation, but it is also one which writers find most difficult. Perhaps because those to whom dialogue comes most easily choose to write plays or scripts, novelists in training always groan when their tutor suggests a dialogue exercise.

An ear for dialogue is thought of as a natural gift. If you don't have it, make do with the ears you have. Writing dialogue well means first of all listening, to what people say, how they say it, and what they mean. Good dialogue writers are compulsive eavesdroppers – Maeve Binchy even taught herself to lipread so she could follow a fascinating conversation across a crowded room.

Listen to the way people talk. Notice their verbal patterns, their turns of phrase, the size of their vocabulary, the strength of their syntax, the little shreds of their cultural background, the distant echoes of their parents' favourite sayings.

Notice the verbal patterns of domination and submission, how controlling personalities criticise, destabilise and assume control in talk, while their victims agree, placate and apologise.

Notice gender differences. Women are big on rhetorical questions: 'How could you do a thing like that?' Men like the sweeping statement: 'That's the stupidest idea I've ever heard.'

Notice how emotion comes out in speech. Anger is easy – it keeps Quentin Tarantino in business; constant swearing means constant anger, the product of frustration. Anxiety is all about questions: 'Where can I park?' 'Do I look OK in this dress?' 'Have you got the tickets?' Love is most readily expressed by people who can't feel it. The film *Four Weddings and a Funeral* would have been a ninety-second commercial for the English Tourist Board if the hero had been able to say 'I love you'.

Notice how people consciously project their own identities in their speech, using the slang and jargon they think is right for the role they have chosen to play: – 'As if!', 'OK, give me a ball-park figure', 'Enough already!'

Notice how confrontational people are prepared to be; in the face of an outrageous suggestion one person will blank and say, 'Oh, well, if you really think so.' Another person will try, 'That's a *very* interesting idea, I'm just wondering if *you* would feel comfortable with something which in some ways might be considered to amount to deliberately causing a death,' whilst a third might storm right in with, 'Murder? Are you out of your fucking mind?'

While you observe all this, digest it and forget it. The words you need to put in your characters' mouths should not be natural speech, but something evocative of it. You need to give each person an individual voice, but also make the dialogue work in the story.

You also need to bring a great deal of what in natural conversation is subtext up to the surface. This is a major difference between a novel and a script. Novelists who write for the screen are inclined to produce over-written dialogue at their first attempt, because they are unused to considering what will take place in the spaces between words.

Readers can imagine a lot, but they can't see the faces that go with sarcasm, evasion or deliberate understatement. In common with the rest of the text, your characters' speech should be immediately comprehensible, which will mean filling in, smoothing over and rounding out exchanges which in life, a film or a play would be accomplished in a few monosyllables delivered with a lot of expression.

Although the way in which people enter and leave conversations is extremely telling, dialogue in a novel is usually written without the hellos and goodbyes, and without most of the ums, ers, repetitions and the lubricating sentences such as 'I mean', 'I know' and 'don't you think?' which are part of natural speech.

Novel dialogue is also brisk compared to natural speech. The exchanges are relatively short, seldom more than four to ten speeches before a paragraph of description breaks the rhythm. This makes it possible to make minimal use of 'he said' and 'she said' or even cut them entirely. These words are dead wood and there are many better ways to carry on a conversation.

A boy with shoulder-length hair lay on the floor. 'Oh Jingle darling, *could* it be tomorrow?' Connie implored. 'It's not often my oldest, oldest lover comes to see me.' He had forgotten her voice. She played with it constantly, pitching it at all odd levels. 'I'll give you a whole free hour, dear, all to himself: will you? One of my dunderheads,' she explained to Smiley, long before the boy was out of earshot. 'I still teach, I don't know why. *George*,' she murmured, watching him proudly across the room as he took the sherry bottle from his briefcase and filled two glasses. 'Of all the lovely darling men I ever knew. He *walked*,' she explained to the spaniel ... 'Look at his boots. Walked all the way from London, didn't you, George. Oh *bless*, God bless.'

It was hard for her to drink ... 'Did you walk alone, George?' she asked, fishing a loose cigarette from her blazer pocket. 'Not accompanied, were we?'

He lit the cigarette for her and she held it like a peashooter, fingers along the top, then watched him down the line of it with her shrewd, pink eyes. 'So what does he want from Connie, you bad boy?'

'Her memory.'

'What part?'

'We're going back over some old ground.'

'Hear that, Flush?' she yelled to the spaniel. 'First they chuck us out with an old bone then they come begging to us. Which *ground*, George?'

'I've brought a letter for you from Lacon. He'll be at his club this evening at seven. If you're worried you're to call him from the phone box down the road. I'd prefer you not to do that, but if you must he'll make the necessary impressive noises.'

She had been holding him but now her hands flopped to her sides and for a good while she floated round the room, knowing the places to rest and the holds to steady her and cursing, 'Oh damn George Smiley and all who sail in him.' At the window, perhaps out of habit, she parted the edge of the curtain but there seemed to be nothing to distract her.

'Oh George, damn you so,' she muttered.

TINKER TAILOR SOLDIER SPY
John Le Carré

Dialogue should never be a substitute for action – if your characters start rushing on to the page and telling each other what has happened you are giving in to imagination fatigue. A rash of exclamation marks suggests early stages of the same complaint. Unless you are writing frothy comedy, more than one exclamation mark on a page devalues whatever has been said.

Naming Names

What is a name? Two words which express a whole human identity. Perhaps the most important words in the whole description of your character. Could Scarlett have been called Blanche? Would a Cardinal Macnamara have had the same distinction as Cardinal de Bricassart? Would Raphael Ash have been as steadfast as Gabriel Oak? Never.

Names are powerfully evocative, and the central character in a popular novel is often given a name which is very simple, very common and therefore no obstacle to the reader's identification. These names are part of the blank-screen strategy – Annie, Cathy, Emma, James, Jane, George, Martin, Mitchell, Robert.

Some female protagonists have androgynous names like Billie, Monty, Lucky, Teddy and Darby, which I suspect elicit empathy from male readers more easily than something downright feminine. In *Damage* and *Rebecca*, the central character is never named. In *The Day of the Jackal*, the Jackal remains anonymous. Some names, one syllable though they are, are strong indicators of the character's qualities, like Bond, Hope and Harte.

Only the most minor roles in the story can be given to people with names which look unpronounceable. The reader's eye will stumble over Roisin, Boudleaux or Zbigniew and no journey is pleasant if there are too many obstacles. In general, the less prominent the character the more exotic the name they can carry.

Names are hugely evocative, as every parent discovers. Every name comes with 22 pieces of matching cultural baggage. You need to choose a name as carefully as a poet composing a haiku. In Christian cultures, many Biblical names are usefully widespread and so come almost free of associations – John, James, Jonathan, David, Peter, Tom, Andrew, Mary, Anne and Sarah. Less common Old Testament names – Daniel, Joseph, Abraham, Abigail, Leah, Aaron, Jesse, Jacob or Miriam – suggest uncompromising old-fashioned morality; Nathaniel and Bartholomew suffer from childish diminutives. Adam has been over-used in pulp romances.

New Testament names suggest virtue on a more human scale: Luke, Matthew, Mark and Simon have a mild glamour about them although Martha has gone down in legend as the self-pitying drudge in the kitchen.

Helen, Stephen, Anthony and Alex are good plain names, but others of Greek origin have a faint intellectual tang – Philip, Stephen, Chloe and Zoe, not to mention Cassandra and Artemis. Socrates and Aristotle suggest megalomaniacs, and there is an aristocratic frost on Diana. Some names from ancient mythology come ready-soaked in doom, like Jocasta and Electra. From Rome, Julius, Candace, Tarquin, Damian and Marcus are grandiose going on pretentious, Augustus is a figure of fun, Flora is a young goddess. Victoria and Virginia are loaded with implications.

There are the excessively romantic Arthurian knights, Gawain, Gareth and Tristram and their ladies, Elinor and Iseult.

There are the wild Celts like Sean, Tara and Liam, and the tame Celts like Brian, Keith and Deirdre. There are the seductive but perhaps over-refined French – Charlotte, Louis, Charles, Madeleine, Marguerite and Josephine. Hortense needs to be at least 70 years old. Hildegarde and Wilhelmina are outright Valkyries while Ingrid, Pia, Sven and Ingemar only demand to be blond. Carmen will always have gypsy blood. Eve is still the eternal feminine, but Donna has become an eternal doo-wop chorus.

The change between a name as given and as it is used is very telling. Spot the difference between Frances and Fanny, Elizabeth, Lizzie and Bess, between Christopher and Kit, Maximilian and Maxie. In *The Prince* a girl whose parents, socially ambitious but not well-read, had named her Jocasta, grew up to be a bold, clever, independent woman who called herself Jo.

Surnames are as evocative as Christian names and have particularly precise cultural associations. Surnames are rooted in the history of language, often referring to individual qualities or archaic job descriptions. Faint as they are, the echoes of these associations linger, in names as different as Coward and Makepeace, Marriner and Major, Esposito, Caridad and Esperanza. A great many surnames are simply place names; when you have defined the backstory of your character, you can name them by opening a map of their country of origin and searching for a place which has the right associations.

The spread of surnames in a book is a strong indicator of the kind of society in which the story is placed. In *Presumed Innocent* Scott Turow chooses names from a range of ethnic backgrounds which spans the globe. Among the lawyers, police, criminals and officials in the urban Mid-West of America, prosecutor Rusty (given name Rozat) Sabich encounters Carolyn Polhemus, Nico Della Guardia, Raymond Horgan, Augustine Bolcarro, Lionel Kenneally, Paul Dry, Cliff Nudelman, Stanley Rosenberg, Tommy Molto, Alejandro Stern, Stew Dubinsky, Eugenia Martinez, Dr Narajee and Dr Kumagi.

Beyond these names, there is no ethnic shading in the characterisation. These people investigate hideous sex crimes. It is an environment in which love of any kind is hard to find. All the supporting relationships in this story are distant – parents are estranged, friendships are expedient and the only close families are the abusive ones. The lack of cultural grounding in these characters intensifies the atmosphere of desperate loneliness, emphasising the obsessive passions at the heart of the story.

Is it Legal?

Choosing surnames brings the added danger of inadvertent libel. If you innocently choose a name which already belongs to a living person and if there is any coincidental similarity between your fiction and their lives, they may consider that you intended to portray them. People become strangely egotistical in the presence of a book. The 'resemblance to any person, living or dead . . .' disclaimer is not an effective defence against such a claim. An unusual name can be checked for prior ownership with the telephone directory. Alternatively, a name which is extremely common is a safe choice because so many people share it.

Without sharing names, a real person can object legally to your book if it is possible that a character in it could be considered to be a portrayal of them, and if that portrayal is damaging to them. Since a great many novels have an element of autobiography this is something to which an author should be sensitive.

Lawyers are often nervous about people who hold named offices, such as a mayor of New York, fashion editor of Vogue or captain of the trawler *Barbarella*, because if you have identified the position it could be said that you had also identified the holder of it. You may be advised to describe such characters neutrally or positively, so that your description could not be considered defamatory. You may also be advised to portray such characters in ways which make clear that no identification is intended: if the real mayor is a woman, make your character a man, if the real fashion editor is short and dark, make her tall and blonde, if the real trawler's port of origin is Lyme, paint Scunthorpe on the transom of yours.

You may write a character without any intention of basing them on a famous person and spontaneously create a lookalike. It is possible to make it clear that no portrayal is intended by giving the celebrity a guest appearance elsewhere in the story, again in a neutral or positive light, but you may be advised to go further and add a significant difference to your picture.

CHAPTER
9
Style

'Would you convey my compliments to the purist who reads your proofs and tell him or her that I write in a sort of broken-down patois which is something like the way a Swiss waiter talks, and that when I split an infinitive, God damn it, I split it so it will stay split.'

Raymond Chandler

How you write is as important as what you write. The style which you develop determines both your readers' pleasure and your success. Susan Sontag observes that art is seduction, not rape. The author must fascinate, persuade and beguile the reader, gaining her trust, arousing her curiosity, drawing her deeper and deeper into the book, making her forget herself and her external reality as she enters the story and experiences its events. The way in which you write is crucial to this process.

Good writing stimulates the reader's mind, galvanises the imagination and above all offers the pure pleasures of language.

Everyone feels the power of words. Many are also drawn to reading almost as a cult activity, something which confers the cachet of knowledge, sophistication and wisdom. It is a mistake to think of the readers of literary novels as a separate class in this respect – most readers are omnivorous and do not choose their books with regard to any supposed division between literary and popular writing. We all admire verbal skill and we all enjoy a little intellectual flattery. For many reasons, the better your book is written the more successful it will be.

Writing well means developing a style, your own literary 'voice'. It also means learning the techniques of writing for a large readership. A popular writer trains her writing to reach her readers just as an actor trains his voice and body to project to the back row of the gallery. The actor begins with a good voice, the inclination to use it and a love of theatre; he will study and develop his natural gifts. He will learn ways of breathing, moving and producing his voice, the special techniques of speaking in a huge auditorium . . . Eventually he will be able to go on stage in a theatre seating 2,000 people who will be moved, thrilled and enraptured by his performance while hearing every word perfectly. The actor will not stop training at this point. He will think of his voice as an instrument and never stop practising and developing his technique. The writer follows a similar process.

Popular fiction demands the mastery of a lucid, flowing style. That style will enable your readers to understand the story immediately, to absorb its ideas readily, to race through the action without stumbling, to follow the descriptions with interest, to experience the emotions vividly and to sense all the different landscapes – physical and psychological – through which you lead them.

The first imperative is to be understood. Beyond that, many different literary styles flourish among bestsellers. Authors learn to write in a way which harmonises with the content of their stories. Thrillers demand muscular writing with short sentences, short paragraphs and simple constructions. Description is brief and precise. Social satires need something as bright as neon and as hot as hell. Stories of fantasy or emotion lend themselves to lyricism, to sentences which can be elongated and elaborated, embroidered with imagery, coloured with allusions and allowed to resonate in the reader's imagination.

Whatever your genre, it is advisable to err on the side of clarity. If the language of the book obscures its sense the reader will feel that they can't get into it. Your ideas may be sensational and your construction faultless, but if the story is badly written many people will not be able to read it at all. Reading bad writing is like running up an escalator which is coming down, or trying to eat a peanut-butter sandwich with a dry mouth. It is possible but only a small number of people would call it fun. Your story will be totally ineffective if you tell it in the wrong words.

We have noted that books are read against all the demands of modern life. Readers' concentration can easily be broken by an unfamiliar word or a contorted sentence. People read books in short stretches – most report reading for 30 minutes to an hour at a time. People typically pick up a book after going to bed and before falling asleep. Only about half your readers will give a book their full attention – 36% listen to music at the same time, 25% read while eating, 25% watch TV and all parents seem to read while keeping an eye on their children. These are the big readers, the people who buy at least one book a month as well as borrowing books from the library and exchanging them with friends.

Simple language is not necessarily ugly, but nevertheless there is a widespread belief that for a book to be popular it actually needs to be badly written, a belief cherished in defiance of the fact that most bestselling books are decently written, many of them are well written and some demonstrate that literary merit does not disqualify a book from commercial success.

Despite this collective misconception, the better your book is written, the easier it will be for you to find a publisher. Very few executives in the world of books entered their professions with the aim of publishing great popular fiction. Most of them want to publish Nobel prizewinners, Pulitzer prizewinners, Booker prizewinners and authors shortlisted for these and other major literary awards. Their constant fantasy is a book which will not offend their literary taste but still sell millions so that they can carry on taking the people they consider to be real authors out to lunch. Any publisher or agent with these ambitions will read a badly written book with a distaste which will colour their view of its commercial potential.

Reading

We talk of cultivating style as if it were a garden, and like a garden writing needs feeding and weeding. Scott Fitzgerald advised his daughter that, 'A good style simply doesn't form unless you absorb half-a-dozen top-flight authors every year. Or rather it *forms* but, instead of being a subconscious amalgam of all that you have admired, it is simply a reflection of the last writer you have read, a watered-down journalese.' Setting aside the question of whether a 'top-flight' author should use a cheap expression like 'top-flight', it is wise counsel.

Motivation tutors are fond of explaining that the human mind is a machine which works on the GIGO principle – garbage in, garbage out. If you want to write well, it is necessary to read well. Reading well means reading literary novels as well as popular ones, and reading systematically to explore your own mind as well as the minds of great authors. Allowing your personal taste to guide you is part of this process. The more you find to admire and enjoy the stronger your own sense of identity as a writer will become. Set yourself challenges to stretch your understanding, but draw a line between discipline and masochism. If you begin *Remembrance of Things Past* and feel as if you are sinking into a bog of unsweetened semolina, get out before you drown.

While every would-be novelist reads Charles Dickens and Jane Austen, and most would-be popular novelists have the sense to read at least the current bestsellers in their genre of choice, the popular writers of the past are also great teachers. According to your personal taste, Arnold Bennett, John Buchan, Colette, C S Forester, Elizabeth Gaskell, Rider Haggard, Rudyard Kipling, Anthony Trollope, Mark Twain, Jules Verne, H G Wells and Edith Wharton have immense pleasure to offer and great lessons to give, not the least of which is how well popular authors wrote before being expected to write badly.

Weeding

Developing a good style means digging out the useless species which can invade your garden. Not only will these monsters look ugly if you let them take root but they will also smother the beautiful and fruitful plants which you originally intended to grow.

Weeds are biologically very efficient. They are invasive, they seed themselves freely, multiply fast and resist extermination. Stylistic weaknesses invade our writing readily because they litter our memories and spring to mind while we are still working on an original construction. Good cultivation means not only educating your eye to be able to identify weeds but having the patience to pull them out again and again and again.

The more distance you can have from your writing, the easier it will be to see what needs to be removed. While some authors struggle to write cleanly from the start, others delay before refining their prose. Some begin a new day by revising the work of the previous one – which has the added benefit of letting you pick up the thread of your story – while others write a first draft for structure and then rewrite it for style. Some writers also consider some weeds acceptable, but those most generally regarded as pests are:

✗ Imitations
Imitation is something you can set yourself as an exercise – a lot of authors have written pastiches purely to amuse themselves – and it is an unconscious process of study. It can be helpful to go back to another writer's story and see how they tackled a specific technical problem, but when you are writing as yourself imitation will inhibit your own voice. It can do worse than that: however much you might admire James Joyce or Marguerite Duras, it would be disastrous to accept the direct influence of their styles for the simple practical reason that such unstructured writing is too demanding for popular genres.

Love other authors' books, enjoy them, analyse them and learn from them, but take care not to imitate them, even unconsciously.

✗ Time-travellers

In the excellent adventure of your reading, you will meet some interesting dudes. As you travel through the past, especially in the nineteenth century, do not let archaisms such as 'she was obliged to stop' or 'his manner showed a want of courtesy' hitch a ride home with you and mess up your own writing. Archaisms sound *truly* bogus, even in a period story.

✗ Clichés

Cliché is a word from the bygone days of metal typesetting, the French printers' term for a block of type. When letters were cast individually in metal and each letter was picked out one at a time with tweezers to make a word, when the same combination of words was used over and over again, it made sense to cast the whole lot permanently together in one slug.

Every cliché starts life as a really nifty expression, a bright, fresh combination of words putting an idea so exactly, so wittily and so much better than the plain description that thousands of people are enchanted and repeat it until it becomes completely overworked.

Clichés are like cockroaches in New York, they infest everything despite the most thorough precautions and they are so endemic that no one should be ashamed of them. When you are tired, or struggling with another kind of problem, clichés will break out all over your writing like a rash. In the first draft of a passage you may not even notice them, but when you review your work they will smack you in the eye and make you cringe at your own lack of originality.

Many clichés – 'left to the tender mercies of . . .' or 'many topics had been aired' – are pretentious circumlocutions. Some are time-worn metaphors – 'beating about the bush' or 'past its sell-by date'. Others are verbal marriages which have endured too long: 'a measure of truth', 'a shocked silence', 'an irretrievable breakdown'. These phrases have become ugly, but the real harm of a cliché is that it weakens the effect of your writing. Because the words are over-familiar they have no real power to move your reader. A cliché packs all the punch of a pillow. It undermines both the readers' pleasure and the author's own authority.

✘ Journalese

Journalists have to convey the maximum information in the minimum space, which means that they jam facts together without elegance. They also have to grab and keep the attention of readers who are much more distracted than those who commit themselves to a book, which they achieve by using a lot of slang, a lot of adjectives and the most lurid images they can drum up before the edition goes. Journalese is sleazy, colourful, exciting but debilitating to read: 'With her son Wade still under the age of five, Scarlett became the first member of her family to break with tradition and go out to work in her husband's sawmill. In a city suffering increasing racial violence and a post-war slump, the business suffered and the strain of being a full-time working mother began to take its toll . . .'

✘ Pretentiousness

Writers who try to appear better than they are sound pretentious because they choose words which are too grand for their purposes. Since most people want to appear better than they are, most writers get pretentious at times. Tastes in this area differ. A passage which one person will read as precious or pompous will seem quite ordinary to another. If you are doubtful on this score about something you have written, try revising it with the simplest sentences and plainest words you can find, then see if elaboration will add anything. Forget commas for a while. Stick to full stops. Make yourself do those exercises where you write without adverbs or adjectives. Kick your vocabulary and see what it spits out.

✘ Dialect

Your mind's ear may hear your characters speaking Kingston yardie or Yorkshire flat-cap, but the dialogue you write for your characters must communicate the sense of their words. Satisfying as it is to tune into dialect, a statement like, 'Ye'man, me nivah go a none di meeting, me pon night shift allya week, das how life do me now,' may be absolutely appropriate to your character but your readers will double-take on it or skip it. Substantial dialect conversations will kill the reader's concentration. Furthermore, a reader who comes from the same culture may feel offended by the way you choose to represent its speech, even if you speak that way at home yourself.

Readers also have keen ears for the way people talk, and it is enough for a writer to suggest the dialect or the accent intended:

Nico and I had spent hours attempting to prepare Lucille for the testimony, with no visible result. She looked terrible, a frumpy fat lady in a tight dress, rambling on about this awful thing that happened to her ... She was already heading for devastation on cross when Nico finally began to elicit testimony about The Act.

And what did Mr Mack do then, Mrs Fallon?

He done it.

What was that, ma'am?

What he been sayin he do.

Did he have intercourse with you, Mrs Fallon?

Yes, sir, he done.

Did he place his sex organ inside yours?

Uh huh.

And where was the razor?

Right here. Right here on my throat. Pressin right there, I thought every time I breathe he goin to slice me open.

All right, ma'am. Nico was about to move on, when I, seated at counsel table, handed him a note. That's right, said Nico, I forgot. Did he have a climax, ma'am?

Sir?
Did he have a climax?
No, sir. He be drivin a Ford Fairlane.

PRESUMED INNOCENT
Scott Turow

✘ Jargon
'Devastation on cross'. Every profession has its jargon and up to a point those terms add to the appeal of a story's location. Beyond that point, technical phrases in a book confuse the readers. They need to be restricted to a handful and used at first only in passages where their meaning can be either explained or deduced by the reader.

✘ Foreign words
Thanks to James Clavell, the customers of Chinese restaurants all over the world greet the maitre d' as *Tai Pan*. Clavell's Asian cycle of five novels is a long, enthralling and passionate argument for cultural tolerance. In the third book, *Shogun*, the central character sets out to learn Japanese, and the readers learn with him.

'*Wakarimasu ka?*' Omi said.
  'He says, do you understand?'
  '*Hai.*'
  '*Okiro.*'
  'He says you will get up.'
  Blackthorne got up, pain hammering in his head. His eyes were on Omi, and Omi stared back at him.
  'You will go with Mura and obey his orders.'
  Blackthorne made no reply.
  '*Wakarimasu ka?*' Omi said sharply.
  '*Hai.*'

When *Shogun* was published in 1975, the words 'Pacific' and 'rim' were not cohabiting and the scars of World War II had not yet healed. The critic of the *New York Times Review of Books* noted that, 'It's not only something that you read – you live it,' and it was one of Clavell's great gifts to drag a reader so deep into his stories that they are all but experienced as life. This trick with the language was part of it; we learn a few phrases of Japanese alongside Blackthorne. We are bewildered when he is bewildered and as he learns the language we share his sense of mastery.

Unless you have as good an argument as James Clavell and can be equally clever, leave out all unexplained, unfamiliar and unnecessary foreign words. If your story is set in a foreign country, ration yourself to six words of its language – you do not need more to create a good sense of place. Otherwise, use only the most widely understood foreign words. No *Schadenfreude*. No *de haut en bas*. No *¡hola guapo!* No *sine qua non*. Translate them or cut them. *Wakarimasu ka?*

Help

Although authors are condemned to work alone, the most effective way to develop every aspect of writing is with feedback. The writers who dominate the bestseller lists have had earlier careers in journalism, advertising, television and film, where they have had the benefit of working in collaboration with other people. This concentrated interaction with colleagues who are in fact professional readers powerfully refines a writer's gifts. With a director, account executive or editor blue-pencilling your words several times a day, you learn fast.

The best substitute for this kind of feedback – and an invaluable addition to it – is working with a writers' group. In amateur writing competitions, the work of authors who belong to writers' groups always stands head and shoulders above the rest in maturity, style and construction. A writers' group also offers a magnificent boost to your motivation and invaluable stepping-stones on the path to publication. They are not hard to find – most are registered at your local library, some advertise and some are affiliated to national authors' associations.

Writers commonly ask their partners, friends and acquaintances to read their work. There is no better way to share your involvement with your writing, but as feedback the response of someone with whom you have an emotional relationship needs to be considered in the context of that relationship. People who love you are inclined to tell you what they think you want to hear. People who depend on you may have mixed feelings about your ambition to write. The most useful feedback from a friend will come from someone who can be objective about your writing – someone not too closely involved with you and who has no particular interest in the content of your story.

Both your literary agent and your publisher's editor will also offer you valuable feedback. Editors are often too tactful to try to modify an author's style, and you may need to ask directly for the criticism you need. Bear in mind that when someone has read a story several times its initial impact will be blunted. One distinguished comic writer was suddenly told by her editor that her jokes weren't funny. She panicked, then remembered that this was his fourth reading of the story.

Three Giant Lies

1) Someone Else Will Take Care Of This

It is true that an author can have their novel more or less written for them. This author is a celebrity with a huge public profile on which the entire marketing of the book rests. When a football star turns up at a book signing, hundreds of people queue up at the shop. When an author turns up at a book signing, everyone is relieved if there is a single customer there. Unless you too are a major celebrity, no publisher will pay someone to write your book for you.

Some authors work successfully in collaboration. Two, or even three people can write a book together if their aims and ideas are in complete agreement, or if one person is in command of the process and the others are happy to go along with that. The writing never has the vitality of a single person's work, but it can be sound, decent and readable. If the writers have different values, or if they are using the partnership as a substitute for genuine motivation, the collaboration will be difficult. Authors who collaborate happily are usually friends who know each other well and decide together to write a book.

2) The Ego Has Landed

OK, so you *are* a major celebrity, or your disposable income is large enough for you to think about hiring help. A writing partnership is like a marriage, in which a ghost writer is like a mail-order bride. A ghost can be introduced by a publisher or agent, or recruited from an advertisement in the literary press. Compatibility is rarely considered in making these marriages – I once encountered a rock'n'roll legend who was working uneasily with a ghost whose track record was one vanity autobiography of a neurotic professional divorcee. A ghost writer is usually competent, and some are extremely skilled and sensitive, but even if the ghost is an ideal partner you cannot expect him to read your mind – particularly if you can't read it yourself.

3) I Don't Need This Stuff

Regrettably, the problem which disables a very small but irritating proportion of the people who want to write a book is that they cannot write. They have very poor language skills and, when advised to retrace the steps of their basic education, to study grammar, master a useful vocabulary, learn to punctuate and buy a dictionary, they brush this advice aside, acting from an unshakable conviction that there is some simple magic trick to writing which the author offering the advice is meanly keeping to herself. There is no trick. There is only work, and in writing as in any other subject those last in the queue when natural aptitude was handed out have to work harder. Believing that you will write a book one day if someone just tells you how is like imagining that you will be able to play the guitar if someone just tunes it for you. That's not the way it works.

PART
3

Ambition in Action

10

Writing as an Endurance Sport

'It is not because things are difficult that we do not dare; it is because we do not dare that they are difficult'

Seneca

Part of the mystique of writing is that it is hell. The picture of Chatterton, suicidal in his garret, lies before us all as an ideal. Writers are eager to tell you what torture the whole business is, somehow it confirms their authenticity. I suffer, therefore I am a real writer. Martin Amis likened the process to pulling out your entrails through your nostrils with a button hook.

Writing which demands that you disembowel yourself emotionally is certainly painful, depressing and conducive to suicide; equally the process can be cathartic, liberating, revelatory and much cheaper than psychotherapy. It would be misguided to assume that, because popular fiction is thought of as entertainment, its creation never involves that kind of pain, which is inevitable in any creative work of integrity. The comparison to childbirth is fairly made here, because once that pain has been endured it is, in most but not all sufferers, transmuted by a kind of post-partum euphoria into a faint, heroic memory. The process is nature's way of ensuring that you'll do it again.

There is an important distinction to be made between pain and fear, and much of the suffering which writers claim derives not from mining their subconscious, but from the fear that there may be nothing in it worth extracting. We are afraid to begin, afraid to continue, afraid to finish, afraid to be read, afraid of not living up to our own dreams, afraid that our thoughts are of no consequence to anyone else. Even a fine and acclaimed writer can be afraid of having no thoughts worth putting into words: Kenneth Tynan proclaimed that, 'Every writer, without exception, is a masochist – a depressed person constantly haunted by the fear of unproductivity.'

The greatest barrier between wishing and writing is made of these fears. Nobody talks to writers about self-confidence, motivation or time-management – these are the tools of the commercial world, and the notion of artistic licence allows writers to believe that motivation has nothing to do with their lofty ambitions. Authors, who work entirely alone, must be among the least disciplined of all artists. An unpublished writer has no reason at all to sit down at a desk and work other than the ephemeral notion that it might be worthwhile in the end.

The fear of unproductivity had no chance to take root in my mind while I was working on a newspaper, writing a daily television column which had to be delivered by 4.30pm if I wanted to stay employed. Across the room five eager sub-editors, longing to get away to their partners, squash games or better-paid night-shifts elsewhere, cast anxious glances at me all afternoon until the words were in their hands. If I didn't produce I lost my job. Motivation was never a problem.

Despite the uproar of the newsroom, the operatic arguments, the ringing of a hundred telephones, the TV news bulletins, the distractions of office politics and romances, the dozens of colleagues with beguiling stories to tell, writing at home by myself was more difficult. Accustomed to concentrating against distractions, at first I wrote my books with the radio playing to give me the illusion of company. Work done in solitude seems harder to most temperaments.

Writing a book is not the only long-term task which must

be accomplished alone. Its unique problem is the mystique of pain and difficulty, which prevents writers from seeing problems of motivation for what they are. People study for exams alone, get fit for sports alone, lose weight by themselves, kick addictions on their own. The techniques which are taught for all these solitary long-term achievements can equally be applied to writing. From my own experience and the skilled training of several professionals, notably Jinny Ditzler, I have developed a six-point motivational system.

1) Commitment

Iris Murdoch likened beginning a book to getting married: 'One should never commit oneself until one is amazed at one's luck.' In other words, fall in love. You will have to live on intimate terms with your book for months and perhaps years, and there will be many moments when superficial enchantment has faded and you will despair. If your commitment to the book is strong you will be able to go on until your good feelings regenerate, each time more powerfully than before.

Robert Louis Stevenson wrote of falling in love with his first novel. During a wet sojourn at Braemar he kept a schoolboy painter company at his easel:

> One of these occasions I made a map of an island; it was elaborately and (I thought) beautifully coloured; the shape of it took my fancy beyond expression; it contained harbours that pleased me like sonnets; and with the unconsciousness of the predestined, I ticketed my performance 'Treasure Island' ... No child but must remember laying his head in the grass, staring into the infinitesimal forest and seeing it grow populous with fairy armies. Somewhat in this way, as I paused upon my map of Treasure Island, the future character of the book began to appear there visibly among imaginary woods, and their brown faces and bright weapons peeped out upon me from unexpected quarters, as they passed to and fro, fighting and hunting treasure, on those few square

inches of a flat projection. The next thing I knew I had some papers before me and was writing out a list of chapters. How often have I done so, and the thing gone no further! But there seemed elements of success about this enterprise.

ESSAYS IN THE ART OF WRITING

Commitment is rooted in the book's significance to your own story; it will spring from your own psychology. The act of choosing a book feels instinctive; it can seem as if the book is choosing you. A scene, an incident, a snatch of dialogue or a facet of a character gets its fangs in your neck and will not let go. You find it filtering into your mind almost before you are awake in the morning, running under your thoughts all day, elaborating itself during any moment of reverie.

As with love, looking for the ideal is the best way not to find it. The writer's equivalent of some enchanted evening, somewhere across a crowded room, is the storytelling that is part of daily life, the snippets of narrative encountered in gossip, jokes, other people's lives, news stories, idle fantasies and the things which happen to you. Your imagination will be caught by a fragment of a life history or an overheard conversation in a bar; a few weeks later the scene will still be with you and you will begin to weave something from it.

The spark for my first novel, *Pearls*, was the relationship between one of my friends and his much older brother. My friend had been made redundant; he had always been an excellent writer, wasted in writing the wittiest reports in his company, and after three bottles of Valpolicella we decided that this was an excellent opportunity for *him* to write a novel. I grabbed a piece of paper and outlined a plot which, I reasoned condescendingly, would be rooted in his own life – a story about two brothers, set in Hong Kong where he had lived for seven years.

My friend wrote a first chapter, was offered a new and better job and abandoned his budding writing career. I found that the story would not leave my mind. It was intriguing to turn it over and over, developing it this way or that way, mating it to ideas which also fascinated me. Most of these related to women's lives, and eventually I tried the story as a tale of two sisters. Immediately I had a sense that almost the entire book was there in sharp focus and full colour, only waiting to be projected into words. I called my friend and asked if he would mind giving me my plot back. Only then did I realise that I had drawn that story out of the relationship between my own sister and myself, a source I would never have tapped consciously.

As well as this deep emotional commitment to what for you is the heart of your book, you need to be committed to its theme and its values. If the ideology of your book is something you have imposed on it, if you are not passionately convinced of your underlying argument, if the way the world of your book works fills you with distaste, writing it will be an impossible chore. Think your arguments right through and be very clear about what you want to say, particularly if your purpose is to condemn. A negative theme very readily becomes a negative book. Because you will need to portray the living depths of what concerns you, there must be an element of love in your hatred or you will fail.

Negative characters pose a similar problem. It is as bad an experience to create an evil person in print as it is to be in the company of an evil individual in life – in fact, because there is a tendency to double-dye villains for dramatic effect, it's probably worse to write one than to meet one. In life, wickedness comes disguised by more desirable character traits: fraudulent millionaires are faithful charity supporters, a corrupt politician is a popular party man whose resignation is regretted, a child abuser is himself the pathetic victim of abuse, even Hitler was considered a delightful man by those who came close enough to be fascinated. When outlining the darker characters in your book, take particular care to give them depths and complexities, because if you cannot find some sympathy for them they will be very bad company in the writing process.

There is nothing to fear except fear itself

Suppose you can't raise this level of enthusiasm. Suppose your mind is crowded with beguiling ideas but none of them seems to be The One. Suppose, on the other hand, your mind blanks as soon as you turn it towards the notion of a book. Suppose you feel despair at the idea of ever falling in love with your own creation.

You are afraid.

This is normal. It happens to everyone. You can work out why it's happening to you now and in that process much of your fear will disappear.

The paralysing fear of starting a book can spring from parts of your mental landscape that have no connection with writing itself. Once you have recognised that you are afraid, first review the whole of your life at this moment, looking for recent changes or traumas. Try to assess your stress level – if you have a medical guide with a stress scale in it, find it and see how you rate.

When you are highly stressed, or even depressed, all your positive emotions will be muted and you will have some difficulty in making any kind of decision. In easier times, you will have had no difficulty in committing yourself, but your present condition will probably be showing in the rest of your life now; you may have become uncertain of your relationship, demotivated at work, unsure of where you want to live.

Assuming that you are already doing all the sensible things to take care of your poor stressed self – exercising regularly, eating well, rewarding and encouraging yourself and taking positive action to address your major difficulties – then you have no excuse for accepting stress as a reason to abandon your ambition. If you are undecided between several possible books, evaluate them without sentiment for publishability alone and commit yourself to the book most likely to succeed. If, heaven forbid, you are in such a state of indecision that you can't even do that exercise without arguing yourself into knots, then simply list the ideas on paper, *commit yourself to the will of the universe*, stick a pin in the list and abide by its decision.

If, while you are reviewing your life, it becomes clear that you are someone for whom any kind of commitment is difficult, who is indecisive by temperament, whose focus is always changing, you could choose, for the sake of your writing, to do everyone a favour and go for help to a counsellor or therapist. Don't postpone your book on that account. Start right now.

For any writer, it can be fruitful to explore the possibility that you are intimidated by the high regard you have for literature itself. The more you admire great writing the more daunting the task of writing will seem to you, the more pathetic your own efforts. This is normal even among successful writers: more than once when I have sent other writers proof copies of my work for their comments they have responded by saying, 'I had to stop reading, I hated it because it was so good.'

The fear of not being good enough can appear as a kind of obsessive perfectionism. You may find yourself working a few pages over and over again and still never feeling satisfied, letting the best be the enemy of the good. The book can stick to your fingers; it may seem impossible to finish because there's always a better way to do this or that. That happens when you are afraid to finish. Finishing implies judgement, and that is what you really dread. A creative work can go on for ever, but the longer you postpone your ending the more afraid you will be. If your story really is threatening to become never-ending, you may need to impose an artificial deadline ('If I'm not done by the start of the holiday I'll go with what I've got') and involve objective outsiders who will give you the reassurance you need to consider the task complete.

All these fears are worth examining in depth; there is also a self-help technique for defeating the limiting attitudes which lie beneath it. Set down on paper all the beliefs you have about writing a book, every thought that the idea brings into your head, rational or irrational, from the lousy report you got from your English teacher twenty years ago to Somerset Maugham's dictum: 'There is an impression abroad that everyone has it in him to write one book, but if by this is implied a good book, the impression is false.'

When you have exhausted your stock of self-talk, read the list through. It will be intensely dispiriting, and it represents the mind-set from which you are trying to write. No wonder you are experiencing difficulty.

Having been the devil's advocate, join the side of the angels. On a second piece of paper, write a positive refutation of every single point. You might, for instance, turn around that hack-neyed sneer from Maugham: 'Everyone has it in him to write one book, and a great book too.'

That exercise completed, make a ceremony of disposing of the devil's pleading, your list of negative beliefs – burn it, bin it, rip it to shreds, whatever gives you satisfaction. Get out the angels' list again and, if you want to go the whole hog (you're in this mess, what right have you got to sneer at American psychodynamic ploys?), make yourself an affirmation. But take care, affirmations can be like fairy wishes, you may get exactly what you ask for. 'I have it in me to write one great book' is fine as far as it goes, but 'I have it in me to write great books' might be more useful in the long term, and 'I am writing a great book now' may lack the Maughamian cadence but it does address the immediate problem more directly.

If you are open to self-help advice, *Feel The Fear and Do It Anyway* by Susan Jeffers (Century) is an excellent handbook to employ against fear and indecision, in which the use of affirmations is one of the techniques described in detail. Do not postpone starting your book while you tackle your fear. Start now, and do the exercise at the end of your work period.

2) The Time

The best time to write is not when the Muse is smiling, your biorhythms are in harmony and Neptune is brilliantly aspecting the Moon in your fifth house. The best time to write is a time which is available.

There are writers who write on Sundays. There are writers who write from 10pm to 2am. There are writers who write in the morning and work nights. There are writers who get up early and write before they go to work. There are writers who write in the evening when they get home from work. There are writers who save up their holiday entitlement from their jobs and use it to write. There are writers who take sabbaticals from work in order to write. I once took immense pleasure in awarding a writing prize to a train guard who wrote in his cab between stations. I know people who write on aeroplanes, but they don't admit it in public in case critics say their books read as if they were written on aeroplanes.

'When I first started to write fiction in my spare time,' recalled the American author Adela Rogers St Johns, 'ha! I had a house full of kids and small brothers and some not so small and *they* were more trouble. I got to know more than I ever wanted to know about sunrises. My real work started when everything was *quiet* . . . Thank God, with three hours' sleep I was – and am – okay.'

Books are like children, they need quality time. However, it is up to you to put the quality into the time which you have. This will require sacrifice. There will always be activities which seem more congenial than writing. There will always be things to do which seem more important.

If there is no obvious window of time in your schedule for writing, you will have to give up something you're doing already. Get out your diary, plan your whole week – work and play, hour by hour – on paper, and see what will have to go. Then blank it out and write the magic word 'book' in its place.

3) The Place

When I find an amenable medium, I'm going to ask for a word with Balzac. 'Honoré,' I shall say, after the appropriate words of appreciation for his genius and the superiority of French literature in general, 'tell me something I've always wanted to know. Is it true that you used to write in cafes?'

Balzac wrote about four novels a year, completing 85 works in his lifetime. This argues great facility. He is said to have written in cafes, settled cosily into a corner table with a little coffee, scribbling away while all Paris carried on around him, but I'm not sure I believe it. Luis Buñuel also claimed to write in cafes, but screenplays have fewer words than books. Jane Austen wrote on tiny round tables about eighteen inches in diameter in the corner of tiny sitting rooms in tiny houses which were occupied by four or five other people while she was at work. I have seen the houses, and the tables.

Hooray for them, say I, and hooray for you if you really have such iron concentration that you can write in the mainstream of daily life. Most people need a place to be by themselves and a table, reasonable comfort and light. Kitchen tables are favourite, there's something solid and all-purpose about a kitchen table, as Francesca Johnson knew.

If you are using visual planning, you need somewhere to pin up your schedule, your inspiring pictures and your character cards. If you keep these in a file, train yourself to open it every time you start work. A clock is nice, time on a clock passes rather more urgently than on a watch. If you need to work with notes or research books, try to leave them out, beckoning you; if you have to take them off the table, keep them on something you can easily restore to working position, like a tray or one of those wire vegetable racks on wheels (I would recommend a filing basket on wheels, but the vegetable racks are much cheaper).

What you do not need in the place where you write is any kind of distraction. In most people, the visual sense overrides all the others, so the sight of something distracting is fatal. Anything which normally gets done at a desk will start calling you like all the sirens when you sit down to write, so keep your gas bills and your letters to Australia in another room.

Of course, not everyone has overriding visual instincts: as a very young reporter on the *Daily Mail*, where the fashion editor shared a small office with the great columnist Bernard Levin, I observed a demonstration of his special visual sensitivity. The fashion editor tore a highly sexy double-page photograph from a magazine – it featured a naked black model, a naked white model and a python. This was pinned up above Bernard Levin's chair while he was at lunch. He returned, sat down and continued writing without even noticing the picture. If you can do the same, you will never come unstuck paying the gas bill on the table where you write.

The instinct to get away to write is strong and may be well-founded if you are highly distractible or have a very small home. My daughter and I lived in a one-room flat when I wrote my first book; it was in a block of identical studios, and our upstairs neighbour Elaine, a ballet dancer on tour for weeks on end, offered me the use of her room while she was away in exchange for plant-watering. (Thank you, Elaine – your home made me a perfect office.)

Gazebos and garages are popular. A small number of writers choose to find a writing room completely away from their home, and a large number of writers think this is protesting too much. It was the course adopted by John Braine, who rented an office in his local town. It didn't work for him, he still had an almost total block after *Room at the Top*.

4) Set Goals

For me, this means creating a work plan and a timetable from my working outline. Even if you have no need to finish the book by a particular date – *especially* if you have no need to do that – make a schedule which will cover the whole writing process.

The working outline, discussed in Chapter Five (*see* p87), is a way of story-boarding the narrative, breaking it down into units to be accomplished. The action of each chapter is briefly described, and there are supplementary notes on the theme, the major characters and the metaphorical or symbolic scheme of the work. My working outlines have varied from 3,000 words for a novel of 100,000 words to 9,000 words for one of 250,000 words. (One writer of my acquaintance, who was particularly unsure of her second book, wrote a 100-page synopsis for it and it ended up a shapely volume much less than twice that length.) The writing schedule should be one page only, but should cover the main events of the book. There is every reason to use a chart from the huge range of pre-printed business stationery designed for project scheduling. Your first writing schedule may include goals for the research period and a summary of the research remaining to be done as well as an outline of the plot.

What the writer needs is a way of defining a daily target. You may be blessed with naturally deep concentration and naturally high motivation, in which case all your schedule needs is an end-date. I have only one of those advantages – high motivation – and I need a very firm schedule to get my books finished in the year in which they are due. When the going has been tough, I have set myself two-hourly targets, but for most people a daily goal is enough to begin with. I have an idea of how long I want the book to be and what time I have available according to my publisher's deadlines and my family and other commitments. I also have an idea of a reasonable rate of work. From these factors I work backwards to decide how long each chapter will take and how many days I need to take off for the rest of life. Do not forget personal considerations when you make your work plan – losing half a day because the car needed servicing or you had a hospital appointment will depress you just as much as a morning wasted in daydreams.

There is a distinct group of writers who cannot take any time off once the book is begun, who must storm through to the end in a white heat. Equally, there are a number who complete a first draft and like to leave their ideas to mature in a period devoted to other concerns before going back and revising. Neither of these schedules attracts me, but they may work for you. What works for me is a chart on the pinboard, with nice little boxes to tick off, allowing me to register my progress and keep a word count.

Things never work out according to the plan, which is redrafted several times during the progress of the book. Do not be tempted to abandon scheduling, because you will then lose your sense of momentum in the project. Just be prepared for the work to have a life of its own. Some chapters explode and are divided into two; others will contract and can be merged with their neighbours. Scenes which seemed simple prove fiendish. Your best laid plans do the usual thing. I decided my first book was too long and planned to make my second novel shorter by 50,000 words – nevertheless, it came out at exactly the same length, to the page, and Sally Beaumann has told me that she set out with the same aim and had the same experience.

5) Move the Goal Posts

Your targets are primarily there to motivate you, not intimidate you. In setting your daily goal, it is very important to choose one that is attainable. Being over-ambitious will hurl you into a spiral of discouragement. Once you have your working plan, see how it performs in real life and modify it if necessary.

For the first few weeks, note every day how close you get to the goal, what went right and what went wrong. You may need to redraw your plan immediately. A friend who admits that she is less than a born writer had produced one novel and was working on her second with the traditional goal of 1,000 words a day. Day after day she failed to achieve it and the feelings of pathetic worthlessness, which hit disciplined people harder than flopsy bunnies, grew stronger. Then she watched a television documentary about Graham Greene and learned that in his opinion 200 words a day was enough for anyone. She returned to her book with a target of 200 words a day and fresh enthusiasm, which grew stronger each day she was able to keep pace with the master.

Although a target of a number of words a day is common, it is not essential. You might as well choose to proceed from one place in the narrative to the next; what is essential is that you have a specific, measurable goal every day. You may or may not achieve it, but you will have the sense that you are steadily moving forwards. That sense will grow, and so will your confidence. Each day's work will be easier than the last. The beginnings of books are always laboured, sticky, overwritten territory; the sunny uplands begin when you have a true sense that you are writing, when your characters are speaking their own words and you can take a break for a five-page excursion into something intriguing which has only just occurred to you.

Once you are aware of the progress you are making you can then begin to refine your most effective work pattern and to address the hindrances which may be holding you back.

There is a subsidiary goal-setting technique for more nebulous aspirations. In addition to specific, measurable goals derived quite mechanically from the size of the book and the shape of the narrative, you may want to achieve things which are not quantifiable. Ambitions for literary style, emotional qualities or worldly achievement can be kept before you in a similar way. Never substitute these soft goals for a day-by-day schedule of progress; add them to your work plan. In these areas, whether you do what you set out to do will be arguable, especially in the slough of despond into which writers usually fall the moment they have finished a book, but to have the ideal in front of you will strengthen your focus.

Soft goals can be defined in any way which inspires you. There may be a photograph which expresses exactly what you are striving for, a piece of music which gives you the feeling you want. You could write your own dream review, or create a sentence of praise you really want to hear. You could pick a few key words from your selling outline and keep them in view. If you are specifically addressing an overseas readership, something which symbolises the readers in that country will keep them in your mind – a picture of the commuters streaming off a Sydney harbour ferry clutching paperbacks, perhaps. Whatever keeps your aim in view. I have been known to take scissors and paste to a newspaper bestseller list, piece together the title of my book, my name, a description of the book and a gratifyingly large number for the weeks-on-the-list, insert this entry in the No 1 position and pin a photocopy of the list to the wall.

One ideal to treat carefully is another writer's work. You may burn to write like an author you adore, but their genius may intimidate you. In the previous chapter we considered how it can inhibit the development of your own style if you imitate that of another writer, deliberately or by instinct. Furthermore, you also risk producing a hideous pastiche and being tossed aside by a publisher the instant they spot the inspiration – 'Oh God, another one who thinks he's Thomas Harris'. Put a photograph of the adored one on your pinboard, light a votive candle if you like, but do not read their work while you are writing your own.

6) Get Support

A writer will benefit from the support of three kinds of people. First, a buddy. You've heard of the buddy system, for runners it means a companion to run with, a training partner; for long-stretch prisoners it means someone from the outside world to visit them and relate to them as ordinary people. A writer should have at least one buddy, a person in their lives who wholly approves of their writing, who will read what they have written at intervals – once a week, perhaps – who will tell them that they're brilliant, that what they've written is marvellous, that they're dying for the next chapter. This buddy will also consider the writer to be an ordinary human being; by the end of the book, this may represent a minority opinion. The best buddies are friends, perhaps not close friends, but not people who are intimately involved with you already.

Buddies have no literary ambitions of their own. They need not be geniuses bowed with the weight of scholarship. You don't need any kind of criticism from a buddy, all you need is kindness. To recruit a buddy, consider your acquaintances carefully and put the deal to a likely candidate. Someone with an equal need for support on a long and lonely road – dieting, marathon training – is perfect; reciprocal buddy deals work a treat.

Next, you need the support of other writers. This support is to affirm to yourself that you too are a writer and to help you realise that you are not alone with your struggle, that other people have exactly the same problems as you. Anybody alone with their work gets an identity crisis sooner or later.

Go to your library, ask for the contact numbers of local writers' groups or circles, and join up. Expect to feel intimidated, turned off or weird the first few times, but persist. If the first group you try really isn't for you, move on to another. But join.

Writers' groups read each other's work – groups of writers and actors may do so out loud. Ouch! Painful thought, someone actually reading your work, a stranger who won't be tactful, who doesn't already understand you. So who are you writing for, if not for thousands of people who don't know you? This is precious feedback, and also a great lesson in evaluating criticism. Once you've heard a dozen off-the-wall gripes from fellow-writers, you won't be so sensitive to equally daft comments from distinguished figures from the world of books.

Thirdly, you need the support of your loved ones, your partner, family and close friends. This is the most difficult support to get, and you may have to live without it. But they love you, why don't they want the best for you? If only it was that simple.

A book itself is almost a heroic quest. It is an intensely desirable achievement; there may be envy. A writer is seen as a feckless ne'er-do-well whose children will starve in the gutter; if you are a breadwinner, there may be insecurity. A book is also seen as an intellectual feat, and cleverness makes a lot of people very uneasy – cleverness in women especially, and above all cleverness in wives. The *Educating Rita* effect persists, even today. Ugly but true.

Envy, insecurity and fear will not be expressed openly. Your ambition to write has pressed your partner's buttons, but they won't know that. They'll say, 'Of course, if you really are serious about this, I'll do whatever I can to help . . .' They'll get sociable where they were previously a couch potato, and say, 'But I thought you liked going out.' They'll embark noisily on knocking through the sitting-room wall, and when you mention the noise say, 'But I thought you'd be pleased, you've been nagging me to get this done for ages.' They'll worry about your health, your round shoulders and your shortened hip-flexor muscles. They'll worry about your stress and your sanity – after all, they've seen the picture of Chatterton too. One writer of my acquaintance gave her partner the finished manuscript of her first novel and when he said at the end, 'You know, you *are* a real writer, aren't you?' she did not hit him; however, he is a very big bloke.

The most fascinating Weight Watchers' meeting I ever attended was devoted to the subject of partners and how they felt about it all. Were they pleased to have slimmer, healthier, happier loved ones? No, they were not. They were deeply disturbed by what they saw as the other person becoming more confident and attractive, and they expressed that by undermining the slimmers in the foulest and sneakiest ways: saying the diet was unhealthy, insisting that slenderness was a turn-off and that they loved the blubber, or bringing home a quart of double-chocolate chocolate-chip ice cream, 'because you've done so well and you deserve a treat.'

The slimmer partner represented a major change to the pattern of their lives and they were afraid. The slimmer partner automatically weighed heavier in the emotional balance of the relationship, destabilising the whole thing. So it is with the successful writer.

Some loved ones are fine while you're struggling, but not when you've made it. They claim extraordinary expertise in your new field, informing you that first novels never sell, that second novels are always disappointing, that three novels are the most that any publisher will accept from one writer nowadays. My father, who unreasonably opposed my ambitions to the extent of refusing to allow me to go to university at all unless I read the subject of his choosing (medicine), never bought a newspaper containing my work and used to tell the rest of the family, 'We assume someone reads what she writes, but it is of little interest to us.'

What can you do about this? All the good stuff: ask for the support of the people closest to you at the beginning, continue to show your love for them in ways that they find meaningful, accept their fears, talk things out and listen actively to them in the process, understand. And finally, if all these fail, give up. You are doing something which they find threatening, however irrational that may be. Expect nothing, don't invite negative responses, and shield yourself from sneak attacks. When you're hearing how you're getting a pot belly from all that sitting down and writing, smile and say, 'Yes, you're right there.' Then get up and walk away. How far you walk is up to you.

11

Will Power

You have your idea, the time, the place, your goals, and the willingness to change them. Now all you need to do in order to complete your book is develop persistence. Hollow laughter. Okay, if you could develop persistence just like that, you wouldn't need to read this stuff. Fine.

Are teachers ever taught not to write 'could try harder' on school reports? What a greasy euphemism it is. They don't mean 'could', they mean 'must'. Even so, trying isn't the point. One can *try* forever and get nothing but marks for effort. *Doing* is what's needed.

If your book isn't getting written, it is because you are not writing it. Not because you aren't trying hard enough. Forget trying. Just do it. Will power is like a muscle, it can be developed.

Pumping will power means carrying the necessity of completing your book right through your life and giving it priority over almost everything else. Your book must take first or second place in your life. Nothing less will accomplish your ambition to write.

For a short period I taught time-management techniques and encouraged my clients to set goals in every area of their lives and then prioritise those areas (one of them had 36 life areas, but she was the mother of five). However many goals my clients had, only the top two on their lists ever received enough attention to make life-changing progress. However committed, effective and focused the clients were, they could only progress the two most important things in their lives at any one time – all the rest could only be maintained. The point of conflict was always around the third goal, which was kept at maintenance level because the client just could not sacrifice goal No 2. It is very tough to give your book even second place in your life if you also have a career, a relationship and children.

You have begun work and kept a daily log of your progress. Take a look at what's happening. From the days when things have gone right (if there have been any) isolate the factors which led to your success. You had your home to yourself for an exceptionally long period, perhaps? Something put you in a world-beating mood, maybe a friend's encouragement or a positive response from a potential agent? When you find something within your control which works, make that experience happen as often as you can.

Now turn your attention to the bad days. Time-management studies for business people identify 'interruptions' as the primary cause of lack of progress, and for writers it's the same story but worse, because writing demands a very high degree of concentration, much higher than that required for sitting in an office motivating other people all day.

You need to nurture your concentration and protect it while you battle through the Nine Trials . . .

The Ten Trials

1) The telephone
Can you unplug it? Do you want to? If not, why not? Do you sincerely want to finish this book? If you need to keep your telephone connected while you are writing, make sure that someone or something answers it for you, tells your callers that you are writing, reassures them that you will call back and takes a message. This has the added bonus of making both caller and answerer aware that your writing is important to you.

You are conditioned to leap to a telephone, the ring activates an almost umbilical connection, so if you can lower the volume of the bell, turn it off, muffle it with a pillow or a closed door, do so. Wherever you are writing, you don't need to know if the telephone is ringing until you are taking a long break and are ready to talk. We have already discussed ways of scheduling breaks through your writing time for the sake of nurturing your imagination (*see* Chapter 7, p135). Phone calls must wait until the end of your writing period.

There is a danger that a returned call will spawn more distractions. 'Help! How do I get back a file I've deleted by mistake?' 'Can you video tonight's match for me?' 'Can I borrow a fax roll?' The potential time wasted is awesome. If you're a kind, helpful person you may have to avoid even looking at your messages until the end of your working day.

Yes, you will feel revoltingly self-important adopting these measures, but they must be taken, unless you truly belong to the tiny minority of people who really can ignore the phone. The only situation in which you really need to answer the telephone is the serious illness of someone you love. Every other demand for your availability is unjustified if it interrupts your writing, even the following:

You have just met the love of your life and you're waiting for The Call. *You know how it is with affairs of the heart, you have to start as you mean to go on. If you're temporarily unavailable they'll get the message that you're serious about your writing.*

Your office need to reach you urgently; being unavailable may cost you your job. *Check with the office before you start, let them know when you'll be free to take calls. And send them a fax to confirm it. Writing is business too.*

You are waiting for an important call from your best beloved from a coin-box in a bar in a one-telephone village in Tuscany and it doesn't take incoming calls. *Agree a time at which you will pick up the phone. They virtually invented clocks in Tuscany.*

Your mother is annoyed that she can't get hold of you when she wants a chat. *So whose side is she on? (Need we ask?) Explain that you would like her support for your writing. Keep explaining that as often as you need to.*

2) Significant Others

You may need to get extremely foxy with your nearest and dearest. They may, in fact, be acting deviously with you, although all you can see is that they're bugging you. Granted, they may simply not understand that writing requires uninterrupted peace, but if you have asked for solitude for a period and not been allowed it, you need to think about what's really going on.

There are people who can't stand to have someone they love around without that person giving them their full attention. There are also people who go through phases of possessiveness, and not necessarily only lovers or spouses. Teenagers can get maddeningly clingy during the tough phases of adolescence (are there any others?) and friends can turn neurotic when you are less available than you used to be. Sighing, sulking, moping around, guilt-tripping, developing sudden incompetence – you know the signs. The more time you give to writing, the more problems someone will need to talk to you about, the more meals seem to need cooking, the more essential it is that you discuss this year's holiday *now*.

If there is a way that you can convince the significant other of your affection, use it. Write the you-are-wonderful note to put on their pillow, double up the cuddles quota, buy the flowers. Keep doing it, even after you get a response, because insecurity is bottomless. A counsellor to whom I brought this problem said wise things about primal jealousy, womb envy and castration fears, then admitted that, however sophisticated one's understanding of the problem, there was no known technique for solving it.

Suppose you've tried everything already, that the beloved is still all over you and you are losing your patience. Anger is fine, as a last resort. Sometimes it is the only thing which gets the message through, and you can always make up afterwards. Or not. Writing has broken up homes, but not happy ones.

3) Children

The best place for a child in a writer's life is outside it – temporarily. It is very difficult to ignore a child even if it isn't asking for attention; a good parent always has one ear open for the ominous silence. There is absolutely nothing like the luxurious peace of a home when the children are out of it.

Rather than get ratty with your kids because they disturb you, plan to get them entertained elsewhere while you are writing. All that stuff in baby books about under-twos not playing with friends is rubbish; friends are great for all ages. So are grandparents, the girl next door testing her biological clock and above all the non-writing parent. Many a partner has taken the kids out on a Sunday while the writer writes. It is a lot more pleasant to organise life so that everyone is happy and occupied, rather than choosing a closed door, cowed offspring and resentful mate, and it gives the parent-child thing a bit of structure. The fact that you owe something to whoever takes care of your child will make your time seem more valuable and increase your motivation.

With an eye to the future, however, it is also advisable to do some writing while your children are around. Older children can help you, numbering pages, checking spelling, choosing names. Yes, these tasks will take five times as long as they would if you did them yourself, but the objective is to get the kids on the team.

You will not be able to do your most intense work in your children's company. Minor revisions, making notes, chores like checking, copying files or spring-cleaning your disks may be all you can accomplish book-wise. You will also be educating your children to support you, and teaching them good working habits of their own.

When my daughter was a tiny baby, I put the baby seat on my desk, hung a paper mobile from the ceiling and wrote in half-hour stretches while she amused herself. Then we got to the playpen period, good for 45-minute stints. Next came the imitation phase, the crayons, the plastic telephone and the toy office – down to fifteen to twenty minutes. Granted, I had an angel child who hardly scribbled on the walls at all.

Even after I had someone to look after her, even after she went to school, I still worked while she was in the house. She is now a teenager who has never said a word of complaint about my work and whose application to her own homework is considerably better than mine was at the same age.

4) Strangers

Do not answer the door when you are writing, and don't let anyone else do it for you unless they undertake to deal with the interruption themselves. It is not worth stopping work for anybody who comes to your home unannounced. Meter readers and Jehovah's Witnesses will return. Loved friends who're dropping by will not want to spoil your writing.

5) Animals

You know the score with animals. You're the pack leader, the bigger fiercer alpha beast with whom they wish to exchange grooming and indulge in lovable acts of submission, with a little play-fighting on the side from time to time. The energy generated by writing has a meditative wavelength that just seems to draw animals to you, especially when it's raining or close to dinner time.

Like people, they can be trained. Actually they are easier to train than people. Right now, the cat is sitting on the corner of my desk eyeing sparrows out of the window, the dog is snoozing at my feet and he doesn't even live here. Some animals are very insecure and can't bear to be ignored; if you can't train your animal to be quiet, if it is so restless that it's driving you mad, you must banish it – kindly – behind at least two closed doors and preferably right out of ear-shot.

6) Housework

Don't even think about it. For women, don't even think about thinking about it. Especially, don't fall into the trap of feeling that you can't decently begin work until you've made the bed and cleaned the bath. A few hours later you'll be clearing the gutters and blackleading the grate. I went so far as to tidy the pins on a pin-cushion while not writing this book. Don't start on the chores until your writing is finished for the day. If that should be at midnight, so be it.

7) Errands

Don't do them. Delegate errands to other members of the

household, or shop once a week and include the time in your work plan. Live on pizzas. Stockpile toilet rolls and, if you run out, put up with it until someone else buys them. If you find going out particularly distracting, if a quick trip to the post office is liable to turn into a safari to the supermarket five miles away because – good heavens, you're out of peanut butter and the best and cheapest and crunchiest peanut butter is up at that supermarket – don't go out at all until your day's writing is finished.

8) Personal commitments

See the dentist when you're finished. Get the curtains cleaned when you're finished. Catch up with people for lunch when you're finished. If you get wrecked when you go to a party and then can't write the next day, either don't drink or don't go to the party.

9) Hunger

Have you ever noticed how many writers are overweight? And how many more are on pretty rigid diet and exercise regimes? The compulsion to snack is a very common anxiety response. Anxiety makes the stomach juices flow, which feels like hunger. The act of eating makes many people feel calmer. You will waste less time grazing the fridge if you tackle your primary worry – getting your book written. Train yourself to feel hunger as the spur to completing another paragraph, not the excuse to break off and pour your creativity into a sandwich. If you use a word-processor, remember that biscuit crumbs can bitch up your keyboard horribly.

10) Sleep

Assuming that you are not normally one of nature's dormice, and that your room has everything you need to stay awake – fresh air, a moderate temperature, a reasonably uncomfortable chair – and that you are not actually sleep-deprived, jet-lagged, ill or taking any medication which will make you feel drowsy, then you need to recognise that what's happening is that your fear of failure is so strong that you're slipping into unconsciousness to avoid it. Falling asleep can be another more extreme anxiety reaction.

Coffee is good for this. So is even fresher air and an even less comfortable chair. There are many other non-prescription stimulants to try: cigarettes, cough mixtures, essential oil of peppermint. The most effective cure of all is to reduce your fear to a more manageable level by writing on and proving to yourself that you *can* do it, that there is no reason to be afraid.

How To Be Published

Most people in publishing and bookselling read at least 500 books a week, although there is a discrepancy between the meaning of the verb 'to read' among the general public and its meaning in the book trade. Hence:

Agents: reading a MS implies eye contact with the name of the author printed on the top sheet, and the sensation of a six-figure sum as a result of the subsequent cognitive process.

Editorial directors: a MS is considered read if it has not been lost on the way back to the office from lunch.

Copy editors: have a unique ability to read only the words which should not be there.

Sales Forces: the phrase, 'I've read this one, couldn't put it down,' should be interpreted as, 'I remember it from the sales conference and we haven't got a hope in hell of selling it.'

Booksellers: reading a book involves looking at the blurb and the jacket.

Large chain booksellers: reading a book involves looking at the jacket.

Occasionally, when they are on holiday, book-trade people discover the ordinary meaning of the verb 'to read'. They return to their offices as raving neophytes to a New Age cult. Usually they can be calmed by a

reminder that they had already 'read' the object of their
enthusiasm and declared it to be an unpublishable dog.

Adapted from Horace Bent,
The Bookseller, 22.9.95

The problem with being a writer is being a writer. A writer is
typically an introvert. An introvert is happier to live in the
magical world inside his skull than in the dreary world outside,
and the reason that world inside is so exciting is that it is within
the writer's control. Introverts need to learn social skills. Writers
need to learn two specific social skills – selling and networking
– which they find exceptionally difficult, and which is part of
why they want to be writers in the first place.

A young writer submitted her novel for a literary competition. It was a brilliant book, although outside the genre to
which the competition was restricted, and the judges admired
it unanimously and gave it one of the two runner-up prizes.
The writer was an infant teacher in a depressed post-industrial
city. The award ceremony, the literary glitterati, the grand hall,
the champagne, the press photographers – all intimidated her,
and her husband came along to give her support.

A leading literary agent approached her, one of the most
charismatic members of his profession, almost as famous as some
of his authors. She was overwhelmed in more than one sense
by his interest in her work; her husband clearly felt threatened.
The couple went home and the writer signed up with a
struggling young agency who five years later have not found a
publisher for her excellent book. Meanwhile, the other runner-
up, a man whose ego is stronger than his talent, was well
published, highly praised and launched on his career with a big
splash.

I suspect the teacher and her husband are now working on
the theory that life is unfair and literary success is all bullshit.
This may be correct, but it is only a view of the battlefield, not
a plan for victory.

Are You Ready For This?

Because writers are so inclined to burrow into their imagination, asking yourself if you are ready is asking a question expecting the answer no. In fact, a writer is ready to look for a publisher when she has done four things – dreamed of a book, written at least enough of it to prove that she can finish it, sought and accepted feedback, and moved as far as she can into the world of books.

Some authors complete at least one book before seeking an agent or a publisher, often to reassure themselves that they really can go the distance. Publishers are also concerned on this score: a remarkable number of literary executives cannot imagine a book without reading it, and a remarkable number of prominent, successful people, including professional and published writers, accept advances for books which they subsequently cannot finish. Writing the whole book first is a sound strategy, but one which makes the author take a disproportionate amount of risk in investing blood, sweat and time.

Many authors go out to find an agent at least with a proposal, usually an outline of their book and a decent tranche of it, say the first two chapters or the first hundred pages. Feedback is an important element in success and the sooner you get your ideas out in the wide world, the sooner their strength will be tested.

Whatever stage your book has reached when you decide to seek publication, you will need a *short selling outline*, a summary of the story taking up not more than two sides of A4 paper in double-line spacing. Absolutely not one line more than that. As is evident from the passage quoted above from the organ of the book trade, *The Bookseller*, everyone in the business which you are about to enter is swamped with words. The more concise you can be the better.

You will need to talk to people about your book, which means learning to pitch it – in the sense of making a sales pitch. This means working out one or two sentences which describe the most saleable aspect of the book – not what you are most proud of or what you consider its most important idea, but the one thing about it which will make an agent, publisher or bookseller feel that this book is something that millions of people will want to read. The pitch is a microcosm of everything fascinating in your book, a tiny taste of its treasures. Because it is in itself a miniature story, the tale of how you got the idea can be a very effective pitch, or a verbal sketch involving a key image of the protagonist.

Everywhere you go, if people know you are working on a book, they will ask you what it is about, thereby offering you an opportunity to try out the pitch. As you answer their questions, notice how they react, what they respond to, what makes their eyes light up. (If you duck the question and say, 'Oh, it isn't really a book, you know, just an idea I'm playing around with,' you will not have this opportunity.) Gradually you will form a clear idea of how to sell your book.

There are two schools of thought on pitching by comparing your work to that of an established writer, in the way that the film producers do at the start of Robert Altman's *The Player*. There is no doubt that some publishers are inspired by a snappy résumé relating your work to that of the current bestselling authors; if you feel that there is a genuine relationship between your work and that of a well-known author, by all means take this route. If you feel your voice is unique, do not strain to make a comparison in which you do not really believe. Saying, 'It's sort of a John Grisham-type legal thriller, kind of like *The Firm* but set in a sort of Joanna Trollopey English village . . .' will diminish your book. If those connections can be made, let your listener make them. While some publishers are happy to breed clones, the best have more respect for an author with a good sense of their own identity.

As well as the location of the story, the central character and the bones of the plot, you should give an indication of how you intend to treat your ideas, an echo of your voice as an author. If there is anything startling, contentious, or provocative in your book, you should also indicate how you will handle this material.

If you intend to seek publication on the basis of a proposal, you will also need to prepare a *long selling outline*. This will cover the same ground as the short version, plus a breakdown of the story into chapters and perhaps some notes on the location and characterisation of the principals. There is no need to discuss the theme of your story in an outline, and a great risk of sounding pretentious if you do. Ideas in popular fiction are seldom regarded as a selling point and if you have constructed your story well, a summary of it should give a reader a sense of its theme. The long selling outline should be as long as it needs to be – my first was 33 double-spaced A4 pages for a book of 694 paperback pages, set at about 450 words to a page.

Both outlines should look as handsome as your word-processing skills can make them. A friendly office or copying shop can bind your long selling outline with a plastic spine and covers.

Moving into the world of books means making contact with helpful people. How big a step this is depends on your starting point. Every writer should join at least one of the national writers' associations. The Society of Authors and the Writers' Guild are important sources of information, advice and other benefits from seminars to discounts on books. Both offer categories of membership for authors who have not yet had a book published. An author should also own a copy of *The Writer's Handbook* or *The Writers' & Artists' Yearbook* which list agents and publishers, their authors and requirements, and much else besides of great value. Updated editions are published annually and will be kept in your local library.

Although many authors enter this world like Alice in Wonderland, it is better to be as well informed as possible. Read everything you have time to read about publishing to give yourself a picture of the landscape of the industry. Read a good quality newspaper, the business pages as well as the literary and arts pages, a Sunday if you have no time for a daily. Read one of the two book-trade journals, *The Bookseller* or *Publishing News*, regularly, and read some of the intellectual periodicals, especially when they carry publishing features. If you are particularly interested in an overseas readership, read some of the newspapers or magazines from that territory.

If you have the good fortune to move in metropolitan intellectual circles, you will have no trouble meeting authors, agents and publishers, or people who know them. You can easily talk your ideas over, get feedback, and ask for introductions. If you are in the position of the infant teacher from the provinces, the step into this world is a much bigger one. The place to begin is with your writers' group, to which you should add membership of as many other writers' associations as you can bear – there are a large number of them, mostly based geographically or by genre. Attend lectures and conferences, at which authors, agents and publishers will speak. Join your local arts centre and go to literary or arts festivals – do not forget that your book is part of a cultural ecosystem which includes all the arts and media.

You need to meet published writers and people who work in the book business. Be sociable (force yourself). Be charming, be persistent and ask for help. The speakers at seminars expect you to do this, but please also be sensitive. I have heard would-be writers advised to ask lecturers to read their manuscripts, something which most successful authors are genuinely too busy to do even for friends, but almost everyone is happy to give advice on a manageable scale.

Serious Mistakes

A great many crazy people think they would be bestselling authors if there were not a world conspiracy to gag them. All unknown writers are in serious danger of being confused with the crazies. Any of the following actions will put you under suspicion of being such a person, although most authors make at least one of these mistakes on the road to their publication:

✗ Do not submit a manuscript directly to a publisher

✗ Do not imagine that you do not need an agent

✗ Do not ignore advice you have heard three times or more

✗ Do not expect anyone to care as much about your book as you do

✗ Do not think badly of anyone who cares less about your book than you do

✗ Do not complain that anyone has stolen one of your ideas

✗ Do not use coloured ink or a wacky font

✗ When you deliver your manuscript, do not tie it up with a ribbon and a bow

Finding an Agent

There are two classic methods of finding an agent. The best is by networking. Through social contacts, or through contacts made via your membership of writers' groups, ask a publisher or another writer to read your short outline – not more, unless they ask for it. Then ask who they would suggest you approach for representation. Ask if they would be prepared to recommend you personally to that person. Then write to that agent – or agents – sending your short outline and your CV, with a brief letter naming your kind introducer. For this purpose, cut your CV to one page and highlight anything in it which attests to your writing ability, has inspired your book or would enhance your publicity profile as an author. One New York publicist looked at me sadly and said, 'It's so difficult getting your book on TV because it's a novel. If you were Clare Francis at least we could send them film of you sailing.'

The second classic method is the cold call and, daunting as it is, it also works. With an up-to-date copy of the *Writer's Handbook* or *Yearbook*, look down the list of agents. Some will say they are not considering new authors at present. These are usually the most successful agencies and it is worth calling them to check that situation, which can change. Then make your own list of agents open to new authors in adult fiction, prioritise the list to the best of your ability, and write to the first name on it, enclosing your short outline with a CV and asking if they would be interested in reading more or meeting you. Be prepared to work down the list.

Submitting your book directly to a publisher ensures that it will be thrown on the slush pile and read, eventually, by a young person keen to break into the industry who will have read two novels that day by writers related to the mythical chimpanzee at a keyboard trying to write *Hamlet*. She is already depressed; she knows she can write better herself and a month ago she was at university up to her neck in *Beowulf*. She is probably the last person in the world able to appreciate your genius. Sending your book to publishers without an agent's endorsement is the best way to collect rejection slips.

A discussion with an agent who might want to represent you is at the absolute least a valuable opportunity to hear an expert opinion on your book and on the commercial climate in which you are operating. Be prepared to ask questions, listen, and ask follow-up questions. Before the meeting, ask for a copy of their client list and find out how well they have done for their authors by reading their book jackets, entries in biographical dictionaries and, if you have the resources, looking up their press cuttings.

In finding both an agent and a publisher, think about your long-term aims. If you want to be a dedicated popular fiction writer, your ideal mates are people with a genuine love and respect for your kind of writing. If you intend to write one or two commercial books then move into another field, you may be happier with people whose heart is where you want to go. Everybody loves bestsellers, but some love them for themselves alone and others for the revenue they bring in to be spent on other kinds of book. Think about these considerations even if you have no ambition at all other than to see your name on a book jacket.

At your first meeting with an agent, you could explore the following areas:

✔ their view of the way popular fiction publishing is developing. It would be nice to find an agent with a genuine commitment to popular writing.

✔ their client list

Ideally, they should already represent at least one popular author whose work is dissimilar to yours. If the agency already represents an established author in your area or genre you may pick up crumbs from the rich man's table but there may also be conflicts of interest. If their list is completely literary, or heavily biased towards non-fiction or celebrity non-writers, ask why they are interested in developing a mass-market novelist.

✔ the history of the agency

The agencies most likely to take on new writers are those which are newly established themselves. They will work very hard for you, but with less expertise and fewer contacts than an older house. Some agencies also act for film, television and theatre writers and performers. Their books department may be a new offshoot.

✔ the track record of this individual within the agency

✔ their workload – how many authors they already represent. Try to get a feel of whether your telephone calls will be returned within the hour, the day or the week

✔ what they want to do with your book. The answer to this may be vague, but you will get a sense of where they see the book in its market, and what advice they want to give you on revising your story

✔ their commission rate. This is usually part of their handbook entry, but you should check that figure is still correct. There are minor variations but commission charged is usually between 10% and 15% for home publication and up to 25% for translation

✔ their arrangements for film rights. Some agencies do not deal with film and TV rights at all, some do but in a very random way, some do so routinely and successfully

✔ their arrangements for foreign rights. Some negotiate foreign contracts in house, others act with sub-agents, which can double the commission they take

If you like this person and feel they understand your work and your ambitions, and they offer to represent you, thank God and sign up at once. If you are uncertain, leave the door open and thank them warmly in writing for their time and advice. If you dislike them, or feel their ideas do not match yours, do not sign even if their offer is the only one you get for months. The relationship between author and agent is crucial and can be very close. Trust is essential. Authors do change agents, particularly when they are starting out, but it can be a painful process and damaging to your career.

Why do you need an agent? Because it is a jungle out there and agents know Tarzan from Cheetah. One writer I know was told by his publisher, 'This book is such a great concept that if you don't get on and write it we'll find someone else to do it.' Another writer signed a great deal for a biography directly with a publisher, chucked in his job and spent a year on the book. The publisher was ailing and was eventually merged into another, the new owners reneged on the contract and his book was dropped. Not too surprising, since another biography of the same man was already being written by a better-known author – something an agent could have discovered in the beginning.

Finding a Publisher

It is difficult for any author to evaluate the advice given on any book, let alone a new author on a first book. It is a situation like a first pregnancy, which attracts such huge quantities of advice that much of it is conflicting and the result is total confusion. Your agent's voice is one to which you should listen. They may suggest that you revise the manuscript or proposal before submitting it for publication. Talk through their suggestions to be sure that you understand them, then go to work. If they suggest something which you do not find very acceptable, open up a dialogue and see if you can compromise. The first agent I considered enthusiastically reinvented my humble idea into something so awe-inspiring that I lost all confidence and abandoned it; it was not until seven years later that I felt up to the concept she had outlined.

The polished proposal will then be submitted to publishers. According to the luck and cleverness of the parties involved, it may be taken up immediately or put through a long and painful cycle of submission, rejection and on-to-the-next. In the latter case, keep a diary noting the submission dates and progress matters with enquiries in a respectful but firm tone, beginning one month later. Publishing can be a very sleepy industry and it is not unusual for a proposal to circulate in an office for months while no decision is made. As publishers comment on the proposal, listen to what they are saying and consider making further revisions.

There is such a thing as a good rejection. When I was a very young would-be journalist, I wrote to the editor I most admired asking for a job. He did not offer me a job, or even an interview. His reply was only six lines long, but he complimented me on my application in a way that was so inspiring that I have treasured the letter ever since.

Even so, nobody likes rejection. On the other side, nobody likes writing rejection letters, but a good rejection can not only encourage you but also teach you valuable lessons. Bear in mind that when a publisher declines a book, they usually feel they need to give a reason, but not necessarily the real reason. They might, for instance, not wish to disclose that they are suffering a lean period and have frozen new commissions for six months or decided to cut their lists. However experienced and objective an executive may appear to be, they will also respond subjectively to your proposal, and if it quarrels with their worldview or presents a character with the same name as their mother as a psychopath, they may react against it but pick on something else to criticise.

Books can also be rejected for reasons which you cannot possibly remedy – if you have written a story about an anthropologist in a rain forest, it might come back with the suggestion that if the author were himself an anthropologist the publisher would feel more positive. Never feel bad about that kind of excuse, which probably signifies only that the rejector was too stressed to think of anything better to say.

The rejection reasons to note are the good ones, the ones which seem to be honest, personal and constructive, and ones which you hear frequently. If four publishers in a row say that the book has promise but they don't like your central character, you need to do some more work.

What if they steal my idea?

That is a risk you have to take. A huge bestseller achieves its status by saying something which is already on millions of people's minds. Because millions are sharing the same concerns and experiences, the idea will have occurred to a few individuals at least; the race to communicate will be won by the swift, leaving some of the losers sure that their idea has been stolen. It may have been, or it may not, but there is so much parallel thinking in all creative professions that there is no copyright in an idea. Your only defence against the fear that your concepts may be poached is to make sure that you interpret them better than anyone else, or to have so many ideas that the loss of one will not be noticed.

Publishing Yourself

A tiny but interesting number of authors decide to publish themselves – interesting because the trend seems to be growing, and includes some celebrated figures, such as the Booker prizewinner, Timothy Mo, and Richard Paul Evans, whose book *The Christmas Box* was published by Simon & Schuster after he had brought it out himself. One cookery writer recently published her own book successfully and paid tribute to the imagination and skill of her designer, her thirteen-year-old son.

Printing technology now makes it possible for a self-published book to break even at a sale of around 1,000 copies. The printers chosen are ordinary commercial businesses, not vanity publishers, who charge so much that the operation is scarcely economic. Authors who have taken this route have done almost everything themselves, including designing the cover, getting it photographed, arranging the publicity, generating word-of-mouth approval, taking the books round to bookshops, building up lists of mail-order customers, and setting up stalls almost anywhere – including craft fairs, horse shows and street markets – to sell their product themselves. For these operations, they will have designated a given period of time, after which they will go back to writing. These are people with a quiet belief in themselves, who are energetic, persistent and willing to learn from experience in a fresh field.

Some self-published authors took this route after a long series of rejections, others chose it positively at the outset. They generally report great satisfaction in selling their own books. When a self-published book has sold tens of thousands of copies, enough through bookshops to get onto a local bestseller list, commercial publishers will certainly look at it with more interest.

Being Published

Once a publisher accepts your book, its success is in their hands. What has until now been a story living largely in your imagination will become a product on a shelf which is marketed, sold and bought like soap powder. Even if selling soap powder is what you do for a living, your most useful contribution to the commercial decision-making process is probably to stay out of it until you are asked to participate. Most authors are too close to their own work to know how to market it.

There are authors who have the services of a particular designer, publicist or even editor written into their contracts, but this is usually something achieved when the team has the leverage of proven success. There are authors who have killed their books by insisting on an inappropriate cover design, and there are publishers who have done the same thing.

Usually, a publisher will consult an author about the marketing plan, including the cover design, the cover copy and the publication date, but this is in fact a courtesy. In many areas the most helpful thing an author can do when such a consultation takes place is to talk the decision through so that they understand the factors involved in it then say they absolutely love everything and go home.

There are four points to which you should pay special attention:

✔ the cover design

This is probably the single most important factor in making a book a success. Notice from the responses in the reader survey that a quarter of the people who buy books never look inside them first. The cover will have been discussed at great length in the publisher's offices. Trust them. It was the jacket of *Pearls* which sold one copy every two minutes at Manchester Airport, a design based on a classic *Vogue* cover remembered by my paperback publisher's husband (thank you, Clare and Gill). Books with great covers melt off the shelves. A great cover makes everyone feel great every time they see it.

To the author, however, the cover is often a shock because it seems to have nothing to do with the book. Nobody else in the world will have the same reaction. The cover should be appropriate for the genre of the book and the demographics of its target readers, but it needs to convey the spirit of the book, not relate to it literally.

✔ the jacket copy

This is also important – one of the three biggest factors in a buying decision. Many authors write the jacket copy themselves – yes, even the standard clauses such as 'a master storyteller writing at the height of his powers'. While a certain amount of hype is essential, you should feel comfortable with the way the book is presented. The jacket copy is also an important publicity tool – very often the press release sent out with a book is lost, and a reviewer or interviewer has nothing but the jacket to introduce both you and your work. Critics can be conscientious, but other journalists may not read any of your book before writing about it.

✔ the press release
This is something you may not see unless you ask for it. A good press release sells the book to the media and answers all the who–what–when–where–how questions. It should be possible for a hard-pressed journalist simply to use chunks of the press release in a newspaper without rewriting. Read the release carefully – a mistake may follow you for life.

✔ the publicity
Publicity is the most sociable part of the publishing process, which means that some authors hate it. Publicity can get startling results – I have never forgotten writing what I frankly considered a pretty schleppy article for a pretty schleppy newspaper, about hot new status symbols: the day it came out a man who had been negotiating the price on a pre-owned Rolls-Royce with a very smart Mayfair showroom walked in with my article and bought a new Bentley instead, for £40,000 more than he had previously been prepared to pay.

One of my most extrovert author friends was fairly happy to put on a bikini and sit in a deckchair in a bookshop window doing a live TV interview during a summer-reading promotion. The book sold brilliantly. Talking about your writing, especially in less than requisite attire or on television, can be frightening and the results distressing, but you should do your best to publicise your book, while being aware that you can, and should, decline anything you sincerely find distasteful. Not all publicity is effective, and some books can get blanket coverage and sell zip. But when a lot of people in your publisher's offices are working hard to sell your book, the author ought to be there on the team. Even if your book is ignored by the media, you will build good relationships and learn how to do better next time.
The effort a publisher makes with a book is largely determined by how much they have paid for it. If you have accepted

a small advance, your book will usually be given a small marketing budget, unless something inspires the publisher to pick it up and run with it – such inspiration can be a successful sale in another country, a film or TV deal, the sudden withdrawal of their lead title of the season for legal reasons or just a lurch in the gut.

Months before a book goes on sale, the sales department works hard with wholesalers, large bookshop chains, book clubs and libraries and the publicity department will be working on the trade press. This crucial phase of the operation ought to ensure that good stocks of your book are well displayed when the advertising and publicity initiative begins. Since so many authors are shy and want to devote themselves to writing, they usually assume that writers cannot contribute to this effort. The sales director of my first publisher looked at me as if I had fallen to earth from another planet when I suggested going out with one of the sales reps and meeting a few bookshop managers. If you want to get involved, you may have to volunteer.

Your Film Rights

Sometimes a TV series is born because a producer picked up a book on holiday and loved it. Sometimes a book is filmed because the author is married to a producer. Occasionally a successful actor picks up the book and sees herself in one of the characters. More often a book becomes a film or a TV series because an agent sends it to a producer, whose reader writes a good report on it, or to a scout who decides it has potential.

The reports written by producers' readers would make you weep, and some authors write their own *dramatic outline*, a short summary of the events of the story, the location and the central character.

A book which is already a bestseller is like a product which has been successfully 'test-marketed'. There is proof that the demand for it exists. A bestseller offers a producer a small but guaranteed audience on which to build the whole card-house of funding required to complete the production. A good film or TV series can double your book sales or more – there are, however, a few but famous cases, such as *A Year in Provence*, in which the screen version killed the book.

To make a film or TV series from a book, the producer will first buy an option on it, which is a fee paid for the right to deal in the property for a short period – six months, a year, two years. The payment for this option will be the first on a contract for the rights which can be taken up later when a deal has been done and the funding is in place. 'Buy' is rather like 'read' here; unknown authors are sometimes asked to sign options for no payment until the rights themselves are bought.

You should keep an eye on your competition. If there is already a book somewhat like yours, in particular set in the same location, and a producer has optioned it, he may also want to option yours for a period purely to make sure that it is never made into a rival film.

When the TV series of *The Thorn Birds* was made, Colleen McCulloch withdrew to a remote island off the coast of Australia. This is a course of action I would recommend. You cannot in any sense control the filming of your book. Producers may flatter you by asking if you see Brad Pitt or Julia Roberts in your story and suggesting that your dialogue is so great you should write your own screenplay, but in fact the casting will be in the lap of the co-producers, and unless you are already a good screenwriter your participation will be a menace. Ask the producer if he or she has the verbal commitment of a TV channel to the project and where he proposes to look for funding.

Film deals are famous for not happening. The contract for your rights may mention squillions of dollars, but the time to believe in them is when they are in the bank. Don't even dream of them until the rights have actually been taken up – and even then the whole structure can fall apart and the project die.

Your Career Path

The ambition to be a writer is often formed early and realised late. Before your own experiences can be used in writing they need to be processed somewhere in your being – certainly not in your conscious mind – and for most people it takes years. J G Ballard wrote *The Empire of the Sun* in 1985, forty years after the end of World War II. Some experiences never become available at all.

One of my newspaper colleagues told her university careers adviser that she wanted to be a writer and was advised to marry a wealthy man, but while some rich men's wives do become successful writers, it is not the most useful first career. Good first careers for writers fall into three categories – those which give them the time to write, those which teach them the skills of mass communication, and those which give them the life to write about.

Teaching is the favourite for allowing time to write, and also giving you the opportunity to develop your narrative skills in front of extremely demanding live audiences. If you become a teacher and start a family, however, you will have to consider the demands of your children in the school holidays.

All the branches of the communications industry are good training for writers – journalism, film, TV or radio production, theatre, advertising and marketing are very good training grounds and professions which tend to give up their more mature members easily. Many writers choose literary journalism as a first career, which brings them ideally close to the publishing world but usually means that the time comes when they have to resign a cosy but demanding job for freelance status and the time to write. Careers in the third category comprise all the professions – lawyers, doctors, bankers and politicians are well represented in the bestseller lists, but it is noticeable that many of them have produced books after dissatisfaction in their first choice of metier, rather than planning a writing career from an early age.

The one type of occupation I would not advise is something undemanding and menial which you imagine will allow your mind plenty of freedom. Some aspiring authors feel that they should not commit themselves to any other profession, but put their lives on hold while they establish themselves. They choose to be waitresses, labourers or production-line workers, and some choose to be unemployed. Noble as it seems in principle, this path is so brutalising to the spirit, and in many cases so physically exhausting, that all ambition drains away and a sense of failure and despair takes its place.

Return of the First Giant Lie

To refresh your memory, the first giant lie is: *someone else will take care of this stuff.* Most writers do understand that the Muse is bolshy and books do not write themselves, but do not appreciate how much of the rest of the process is also down to them. There is a distinct strand in the bestseller mystique which suggests that some fairy godmother – super-agent, book doctor or publishing genius – will swoop on an unknown writer and transform them.

Writers with more sense than to believe this would still like to delegate all their business decisions, but shaping an author's career is the final responsibility of the author; the agent can only advise. You may have the most gifted agent and the most dynamic publisher in the world, you may trust and love them more than any other people in your life, but you will still set your own agenda and make your own decisions.

There is also the question of opportunities, such as that which the young teacher had when she went to the award ceremony. Your agent will generate opportunities for you, but two people can open twice as many doors as one. I once heard two magazine writers represented by the same agent in conversation. They agreed that she was clever, supportive and had time to talk to them on the phone, even though she acted for half a dozen immensely successful authors. 'But she never gets you anything, does she?' the first writer said. 'Well no,' the second writer replied, 'but I get most of my own commissions anyway. I need her to do the deals for me, but people just seem to come to me.' One of those two is now a bestselling author.

Appendix

Readers Questionnaire and Analysis

1) Age
Under 20: 7%,
21–30: 40%
31–40: 21%
41–50: 17%
51–60: 6%
Over 60: 9%

2) Gender
Male: 45%
Female: 55%

3) Occupation
Variously: accountant, actor, administrator, banker, bank manager, bank clerk, beauty therapist, creche supervisor, customer services manager, dentist, designer, estate agent, hairdresser, lecturer, lawyer, leisure manager, operations manger, orthodontist, secretary, student, supervisor, surveyor, telephonist, tai chi master, translator, video librarian, xerox operator.

4) Do you live:
Alone?: 15%
With a partner?: 34%

With children?: 2%
With children and partner?: 19%
With other adults?: 19%
With children and other adults, family or friends?: 11%

5) Children under the age of 10?
Yes: 13%

6) How do you travel to work?
Commute by public transport: 51%
Drive or walk: 45%
Work at home full-time: nil
Work at home part-time: 4%

7) At what age did you, or do you expect to, complete your formal education?
Under 17: 23%
17–18: 25%
19–20: 6%
Over 21: 46%

8) At what age did you learn to read?
Under 4: 15%
4–5: 43%
5–6: 11%
6–7: 10%
7–8 or over: 4
Don't know: 17%

Comment: 'Difficult – I read Cypriot first and came to the UK four years ago and started then to learn English.' (Operations manager, 36, currently reading *Far From The Madding Crowd*.)

9) As a child, were you considered:
An early reader?: 47%
About average?: 49%
Late to read?: 2%
To be dyslexic or have difficulty with reading?: 2%

Note: The only respondents remembering reading difficulties as children were now at senior managerial level. 7% of respondents had difficulty with spelling.

10) Would you now describe yourself as:
A fast reader?: 30%
About average?: 64%
A slow reader?: 6%
Dyslexic or unable to enjoy reading?: nil

Comment: 'It depends on the topic – I read novels fast, more intellectual books at average or slow speed.' (Bank manager, 37, currently reading *Truth Tales 2: The State of Life – Contemporary Writing by Indian Women*.)

11) What do you need to read in connection with your work?
Newspapers: 55%
Magazines: 55%
Books: 42%
Technical journals: 49%
Reports: 56%
Other documents: 55%
Plays: 4%
Nothing: 6%

12) How many hours in a week would you estimate that you spend reading this material?
Less than 1: 6%
1–3: 28%
4–6: 33%
7–10: 11%
More than 10: 4%
More than 20: 6%
N/a: 12%

13) Do you feel that you have too much professional reading, that you can't take it all in or read everything you should?

Often: 28%
Sometimes: 23%
No: 47%

Note: Some respondents with relatively small amounts of professional reading still felt that they had too much, while others with heavy reading commitments were content.

Comment: 'I used to be a huge reader, but long periods of concentration are much harder now. I have more professional reading to keep up with – I'm almost saying I've done my quota of reading, all this stuff on my desk.' (Designer, 50+, currently reading *Fever Pitch*.)

14) For enjoyment or personal information, do you read:

Newspapers?: 75%
Magazines?: 90%
Comics?: 2%
Books?: 83%

15) Please rate these activities in terms of which you most enjoy, with No 1 as favourite:

1 – seeing friends
2 – being with family
3 – theatre/concerts/opera/ballet
4 – films or videos
5 – reading books
6 – listening to music/playing sport
7 – dancing or clubbing
8 – reading magazines or newspapers
9 – working out
10 – gardening
11 – spiritual activities
12 – doing nothing

16) When did you last read a book for pleasure?

Yesterday/today/currently reading: 44%
Last week: 23%
Last month: 17%
Several months ago: 5%
Last year or before: 2.5%
Longer ago than 1 year: 2.5%

17) What was its title?

Titles reported included:

High Fidelity
Sophie's World
The Big Sleep
The Rats
Into the Blue
Sugar & Spice
Cary Grant: A Portrait
Spin
Clockers
A Kind of Homecoming
Cellar of Horror
Ageless Body, Timeless Mind
Interview With A Vampire
The Princeling
From Potters Field
Degree of Guilt
Almost Normal
Cleared for Take-off
Nigel Mansell: Autobiography
Queen Victoria
The Vacillations of Poppy Carew
Marabou Stork Nightmares
The Sum of All Fears
The Power of One
The Man Who Made Husbands Jealous
Ruby
A Suitable Boy

Vurt
A Morbid Taste For Bones
Zen and the Art of Motorcycle Maintenance
Mr Murder
Becoming a Man
Truth Tales 2
The Firm
Far From The Madding Crowd
Hollywood Kids
Insomnia
The Oxford Book of Short Poems
A Black Lace Title
Darkness At Noon
Our Mutual Friend
The History of Selborne
Fever Pitch
Trainspotting
What a Carve-Up
The Maid of Buttermere
Lord of the Rings
The Book of Virtues

18) How many books would you estimate that you read for pleasure in a year?
Less than 2: nil
2–4: 17%
4–6: 23%
7–10: 10%
10–20: 19%
More than 20: 21%
N/a: 10%

19) What kind of book do you most like to read:
Answers included:

Fiction/Novels
Light Fiction
Modern Fiction

Modern Culture
Murder/Mystery
Humour
Horror
Biography
Love/Sex
Romance
Historical
Socially based
Saga
Easy Reading
Action
Short Books
Cookery
Gardening
Scandal/Gossip
Poetry
Plays
Surreal
Spiritual
Philosophy
Classics
Reference

Comment: 'I like books to take me into other people's lives or away from the mundane work–home–bed, etc.' (Leisure manager, 27, last read *Interview With A Vampire*)

19) Do you have a favourite author?
Authors named included:

Virginia Andrews
Jeffrey Archer
Jane Austen
Julian Barnes
Maeve Binchy
Tom Clancy
Joseph Conrad

Catherine Cookson
Arthur Conan Doyle
Patricia Cornwell
Charles Dickens
Gerald Durrell
Bret Easton Ellis
George Eliot
Frederick Forsyth
John Fowles
Dick Francis
Reginald Hill
John Irvine
Clive James
Jack Kerouac
Stephen King
Arthur Koestler
Dean Koontz
J Krishnamurti
Lynda La Plante
David Lodge
Alastair Maclean
Erin Pizzey
Ruth Rendell
Sidney Sheldon
Georges Simenon
Howard Spring
Danielle Steele
Barbara Taylor Bradford
Joanna Trollope
Irvine Welsh
Mary Wesley
P G Wodehouse

20) Have you ever read a number of books by the same author? If so, who?

In addition to the authors named above, names given included:

Martin Amis

Dirk Bogarde
William Boyd
Melvyn Bragg
Agatha Christie
Martine Cole
Jackie Collins
Jilly Cooper
Patricia Cornwell
Douglas Coupland
Edward De Bono
Len Deighton
Charles Dickens
Frederick Forsyth
Henry Fielding
C S Forester
Patrick Gale
William Golding
Sue Grafton
Robert Graves
Graham Greene
John Grisham
Rider Haggard
Thomas Hardy
James Herbert
Franz Kafka
Leo P Kelly
C S Lewis
Robert Ludlum
Ed McBain
Alastair McLean
Clare McNally
Armistead Maupin
Nancy Mitford
Iris Murdoch
Vladimir Nabokov
Sara Paretsky
Tom Peters
Rosamunde Pilcher

Lynn Reid Banks
Anne Rice
William Shakespeare
Tobias Smollet
Laurence Sterne
William Thackeray
Anthony Trollope
Joanna Trollope
Evelyn Waugh

21) When do you read? Check as many answers as necessary.
In bed at night: 77%
Travelling to work: 51%
On holiday: 75%
At the weekend: 49%
At home in the evening: 47%
Whenever I have nothing to do: 41%
On long journeys: 60%
In the bath: 23%
In traffic jams: 4%

22) Do you read a book while you are doing something else? If so, what?
Eating: 25%
Watching television: 17%
Supervising children: 8%
Working out: 2%
Listening to music or radio: 36%
Talking to people: 2%
No: 38%

23) When did you last buy a new book to enjoy?
This month: 34%
Last month: 23%
2–6 months ago: 20%
6–12 months ago: 7%

12 months or more: 10%
No purchase or n/a: 6%

24) **Where did you buy it?:**
Supermarket: 3%
Newsagent/corner shop: 10%
Large bookstore: 58%
Small independent bookshop: 10%
Airport or station bookshop: 19%

25) **Was it an impulse buy?**
Yes: 55%
No: 45%

26) **If you wanted a particular book, would you order it from a bookshop?**
Yes: 85%
No: 15%

Note: Those least likely to order a book were in the youngest age groups.

27) **Do you ever buy second-hand books?**
Yes: 71%
No: 39%

28) **Do you borrow books from a library?**
Often: 15%
Sometimes: 46%
Never: 39%

29) **With friends, do you ever lend or borrow books?**
Often: 30%
Sometimes: 55%
Never: 15%

30) When you buy a new book, what do you feel influences your choice most? Number answers in order of importance, with No 1 as the most important.

1 – liking the author's other books
2 – word-of-mouth recommendation
3 – reading the cover
4 – a book review
5 – the cover design
6 – interview or other publicity
7 – enjoying film or TV adaptation
8 – price cuts
9 – advertising

31) Before you buy, do you:

Flick through the book looking for interesting bits?: 36%
Read the beginning?: 30%
Read the end?: 4%
Read one or more extracts from the middle?: 8%
None of the above?: 25%

32) When you read for pleasure, how long do you usually read for?

Under 15 minutes: 2%
15–30 minutes: 13%
30 minutes to 1 hour: 53%
More than 1 hour: 32%

33) Do you finish every book that you start?

Always: 26%
Usually: 70%
Sometimes: 2%
Rarely: 2%

34) What will make you break off and stop reading a book?

External reasons:
Tiredness, falling asleep: 28%

Interruptions: 8%
No time/work/having chores to do: 17%

Reasons in the book:
Bored, slow plot, not catching imagination: 26%
Too complex, losing concentration: 10%
Bad writing: 4%
First chapter not gripping: 8%
Bad characters, can't relate to characters: 10%
Unreal plot: 2%

Nothing: 2%
N/a: 8%

35) Would you like to read for pleasure more than you do at the moment?
Yes: 94%
No: 6%

36) Did you read more when you were younger?
Yes: 64%
No: 36%

37) Do you expect to read more when you are older?
Yes: 84%
No: 16%

Comment: 'I get tired now, so probably not, but I am doing more studying and will therefore have to try a bit harder.' (Secretary, 53, reading *Pride and Prejudice*.)

38) How many books do you own?
Less than 10: nil
11–30: 8%
31–100: 21%
More than100: 57%

More than 1000: 11%
N/a: 3%

Comments: 'Not many, usually borrow from library.' (Secretary, 25, currently reading *The Vacillations of Poppy Carew*.)

'When I finish a book I pass it round or collect them and send to my sons' school for sale – I can never read a book twice.' (Operations Manager, 37)

Further Reading

Fiction

Adams, Douglas. *The Hitchhiker's Guide To The Galaxy*, Pan, 1979.

Austen, Jane. *Pride and Prejudice.*

Ballard, J G *Empire of the Sun*, William Collins/Grafton, 1985.

Baum, Vicki. *Grand Hotel*, Queensway, 1931.

Benchley, Peter. *Jaws*, Andre Deutsch/Pan, 1975.

Brayfield, Celia.
  Pearls, Chatto & Windus/Penguin, 1987.
  The Prince, Chatto & Windus/Penguin, 1990.
  White Ice, Viking/Penguin, 1993.
  Harvest, Viking/Penguin, 1995.

Bronte, Emily. *Wuthering Heights.*

Clavell, James.
  King Rat, Michael Joseph, 1962.
  Shogun, Hodder & Stoughton, 1975.

Collins, Jackie.
  Hollywood Wives, William Collins/Pan, 1983.
  Hollywood Husbands, Pocket Books, 1987.

Crichton, Michael. *Jurassic Park*, Random Century, 1991.

Deighton, Len. *Close-Up*, William Collins/Grafton Books.

Du Maurier, Daphne. *Rebecca*, Victor Gollancz, 1938.

Fleming, Ian.
  Casino Royale, Jonathan Cape, 1953.

Goldfinger, Jonathan Cape, 1959.

The Man With The Golden Gun, Jonathan Cape, 1965.

Forsyth, Frederick. *The Day of the Jackal*, Hutchinson/Corgi, 1971.

Goldsmith, Olivia. *The First Wives' Club*, Heinemann/Mandarin, 1992.

Golon, Sergeanne. *Angelique, Books I and II*, Heinemann/Pan, 1962.

Grisham, John.

The Firm, Century/Arrow, 1991.

The Pelican Brief, Century/Arrow, 1992.

Harris, Robert. *Fatherland*, Hutchinson/Arrow, 1992.

Hart, Josephine. *Damage*, Chatto & Windus, 1991.

Krantz, Judith. *Scruples*, Futura, 1978.

Mistral's Daughter, Corgi, 1984.

Le Carré, John. *Tinker, Tailor, Soldier, Spy*, Hodder & Stoughton/Pan, 1974.

Lucas, George. *Star Wars*, Ballantine/Sphere, 1976.

McCarthy, Mary. *The Group*, Weidenfeld & Nicholson/Penguin, 1963.

McCullough, Colleen. *The Thorn Birds*, Macdonald/Futura, 1977.

Miller, Sue. *The Good Mother*, Dell, 1986.

Mitchell, Margaret. *Gone With The Wind*, Macmillan, 1936.

Tan, Amy. *The Joy Luck Club*, Heinemann/Minerva, 1989.

Turow, Scott. *Presumed Innocent*, Bloomsbury/Penguin, 1987.

Waller, Robert James. *The Bridges of Madison County*, Mandarin, 1992.

Non-ficton

Beauman, Nicola. *A Very Great Profession*, Virago, 1983.

Bettelheim, Bruno. *The Uses of Enchantment*, Thames & Hudson, 1976.

Cameron, Julia. *The Artist's Way*, Souvenir Press/Pan Books, 1994.

Campbell, Joseph.

The Hero With A Thousand Faces, Princeton Univ. Press, 1949.

The Transformations of Myth Through Time, Harper & Row, 1990.

Estes, Clarissa Pinkola. *Women Who Run With The Wolves*, Rider, 1992.

Fitzgerald, F. Scott. *Letters*, Ed. Andrew Turnbull, Bodley Head/Penguin, 1963.

Forster, Margaret. *Daphne du Maurier*, Chatto & Windus, 1993.

Jung, Carl Gustav. *Collected Works*, Princeton Univ. Press.

McKee, Robert. *Story Structure*, HarperCollins, 1996.

(Robert McKee's Story Structure Course, International Forum, The Oast House, Plaxtol, Sevenoaks, Kent TN15 0QG. Tel: 01732 810925.)

Maugham, W. Somerset. *The Summing Up*, Heinemann, 1938.

Mitchell, Margaret. *Gone With the Wind Letters*, Ed. Richard Harwell, Sidgwick & Jackson, 1987.

St Johns, Adela Rogers. *Some Are Born Great*, Doubleday/Signet, 1974.

Singer, June. *Boundaries of the Soul*, Doubleday/Anchor, 1987.

Sontag, Susan. *The Pornographic Imagination*, 1967.

Stevenson, Robert Louis. *Essays in The Art of Writing*, Chatto & Windus, 1908.

Warner, Marina. *From the Beast to the Blonde*, Chatto & Windus, 1994.

Acknowledgements

The author and publisher are grateful to the following for permission to reproduce copyright material:

Alfred A Knopf Inc: *Jurassic Park* by Michael Chrichton
André Deutsch Ltd: *Jaws* by Peter Benchley
The Bookseller
Bloomsbury Publishing PLC: *Presumed Innocent* by Scott Turow
Chatto & Windus: *Damage* by Josephine Hart
The Estate of Daphne Du Maurier: *Rebecca* by Daphne Du Maurier
HarperCollins Ltd: Close-Up by Len Deighton; *Hollywood Wives* by Jackie Collins; *Hollywood Husbands* by Jackie Collins
William Heinemann Ltd: *The First Wives Club* by Olivia Goldsmith
Hodder & Stoughton Ltd: *Shogun* by James Clavell
Hutchinson Books: *The Joy Luck Club* by Amy Tan
Little Brown: *The Thorn Birds* by Colleen McCulloch
Michael Joseph Ltd: *King Rat* by James Clavell; *Tinker Tailer Soldier Spy* by John Le Carré
Glidrose Publications Ltd: *Casino Royale* by Ian Fleming, © Glidrose Productions Ltd, 1953; *Goldfinger* by Ian Fleming, © Glidrose Productions Ltd, 1959; *The Man With The Golden Gun*, © Glidrose Productions Ltd, 1965
Peters Fraser & Dunlop Group Ltd: *Fatherland* by Robert Harris

Random House UK Ltd: *The Day of the Jackal* by Frederick Forsyth

Sinclair Stevenson: *The Bridges of Madison County* by Robert James Waller

Victor Gollancz: *Empire of the Sun* by J G Ballard

The author would also like to thank David Croser, Rodney Fitch, Gill Forster, Adrian Forster, Joy Lamplugh, Sarah Lloyd, Mary Pinosa and Richard Pownall for their help in distributing questionnaires, with thanks to Mary also for her assistance in collating the results. For valuable advice I am indebted to Clare Hershman and, as ever, to Andrew and Margaret Hewson. For their wonderful enthusiasm, commitment, tact and patience. I am deeply grateful to all at Fourth Estate, especially my editor, Jane Carr, and to Emma Rhind-Tutt. Special thanks are due to Andrew Billen, who first suggested this book to us.